LOGAN AND CRESAP,

AN

HISTORICAL ESSAY

BY

BRANTZ MAYER.

ALBANY:

JOEL MUNSELL.

1867.

Badgley Publishing Company
2011

PREFACE

I was invited in the spring of 1851 to deliver the Annual Address before the Maryland Historical Society, and took the story of Logan the Indian and Cresap the Pioneer, as a subject worthy of elucidation. I adopted this subject, not only because the history of Logan's speech, which has given celebrity to both these persons, was likely to secure the attention of an audience, but because, while it afforded an opportunity to vindicate the reputation of a patriotic Marylander, it enabled me also to expose the danger of considering as always unquestionable what are called the *facts* of history, and to inculcate the caution with which we should receive or record the condemnation of individuals. The fact that this essay was originally intended for delivery and not for the closet, will account for the oratorical style in parts of the present publication.

For ninety years "Logan's speech" has been repeated by every schoolboy and admired by every cultivated person as a gem of masculine eloquence. Unluckily, it did not rehearse the Indian's wrongs and revenge alone. It gave point to its artless rhetoric by charging those wrongs, and imputing the frightful results of that revenge, to Michael Cresap; and, in proportion as both were dreadful in character and poignant in statement, the hatred of mankind for the alleged perpetrator became intense and lasting. The speech, it is well known, was first published in the newspapers of America in 1774, after Lord Dunmore's treaty at Camp Charlotte; but its remarkable popularity was secured by the importance given to it by Mr. Jefferson, as illustrating Indian character and genius, by its publication, with comments, in his *Notes on Virginia*. Accordingly, every American, and multitudes of educated Europeans, learned to pity Logan and to hate the name of Cresap; yet Cresap certainly never deserved their opprobrium, and it is quite possible their sympathetic compassion for Logan might have been considerably mitigated.

When I began my narrative I possessed sufficient proof to exculpate the Maryland Pioneer completely; but the subject grew as I studied it; one authority pointed to another, and one topic led me insensibly to kindred studies. Printed works were soon exhausted, and manuscripts became necessary and were obtained. I found it impossible to tell the whole story with proper precision and breadth, without the introduction of illustrative characters and events, so that what was at first intended for a brief discourse, expanded into a paper on the Pioneer life and Indian history of the period.

The discourse, produced with all the care I could bestow on it in the two months allowed for its preparation, was read to the society on the 15th of May, 1851, and was printed in a small edition for private circulation among our members and their friends. From the nature of the facts newly disclosed, its publication in this manner excited more attention than I expected, so that the edition was soon exhausted by the demands of historical collectors. It has been long out of print. Lately, new illustrative information, in considerable quantity, has been received by me, which may be judiciously added; and a fresh edition being asked for, I have carefully revised the whole and recast some of the passages, so as to give the paper — what in truth it should have had in the beginning—the character of a historical essay, rather than an oration.

The main authorities for the thorough vindication of Michael Cresap's memory are the extremely rare little volume of Jacob's *Life of Cresap,* published in 1826, at Cumberland, Maryland, and the letter of General George Rogers Clark, published in the first edition of my discourse, but now *first printed from the original MS.* in appendix No. 1, of this volume. In the edition of this narrative published in 1851, General Clark's letter was printed as sent to me by Mr. Lyman C. Draper. It was then charitably surmised that Mr. Jefferson, for whose enlightenment the letter was written, had never received this vindication, inasmuch as he neither published nor alluded to it in any edition of his *Notes on Virginia,* issued after the veracity of Logan's speech was attacked by Luther Martin, the eminent attorney general of Maryland. But the belief entertained in 1851 became no longer possible, when it was discovered, a few years ago, that Mr. Jefferson's manuscript collections, deposited in the department of state at Washington, not only contained the original letter of General George Rogers Clark to Dr. Brown, vindicating Cresap, but also, Dr. Brown's letter to Mr. Jefferson, under date of Sept., 4th, 1798, *transmitting the paper to the distinguished statesman, two years before he published his testimony in regard to the Logan speech in the appendix to his Notes on Virginia, issued in* 1800.

It would be useless to speculate on the causes of Mr. Jefferson's failure to insert or allude to this letter, for all who could speak authoritatively on the subject, are long since dead. Martin, who was married to a daughter of Capt. Michael Cresap, had attacked Jefferson severely for the slur on his father-in-law's memory; but Martin was a federalist. Jefferson had felt the sting of Martin's publications against him, as is shown in his letter to Governor Henry, of Maryland; but Jefferson was a democrat. It is not improbable that party feeling — then quite as venomous as in later days — may have swayed Jefferson's mind from the justice that should govern historians in regard to even the humblest of whom they write. His omission of this letter is more remarkable and less pardonable, because General Clark had said, "I shall relate the incidents that gave rise to Logan's suspicion, and *will enable Mr. Jefferson to do justice to himself and the Cresap family, by being made fully acquainted with the facts."* But the cautious warning seems to have been disregarded; for in 1800, Cresap had been already twenty-four years in his grave; while the minute, cumulative, lawyer-like pleadings of Appendix iv, to the *Notes on Virginia,* though slightly modifying the original charge, still tended to exhibit Cresap in an odious light, and to show the rankling of personal animosity. Indeed, the suppression is rather to be regretted on Mr. Jefferson's account than Cresap's. For, though the original manuscript of General Clark's complete exculpation of the Pioneer, appears only at this late day, the place in which it is detected, discloses the statesman's decided reluctance to justify the dead, even under friendly monition and invocation. It is a sad picture of the infirmity of a nature which was not proof against political passion, and was known to be ambitious, at least, of seeming to be never mistaken.

The exceptions taken by a few critics to my first publication of this narrative were two-fold. It was thought by some, that I had written too much as an advocate of Cresap, and so placed him higher in the scale than he deserved; and by others, that I had, perhaps unconsciously, attempted to underrate the character of Logan. My intention was to do neither. I had no personal interest in the Pioneer or his family. I did not even know his kindred or descendants; while, I confess, it was hard to free my mind from its early, habitual sympathy with the Indian, so as to write of him with pure and simple justice. I hope, therefore, I have not been, either in my original publication, or the present one, the attorney of Cresap, or the slanderer of Logan. Both these persons are to be measured by the standards of their time and place, for both were representative men. Civilization is to be mercifully and charitably — if not always justly —weighed in the balance of its particular time and locality. Let us consider these.

The time was nearly a century ago; the place a wilderness in America; the actors, an untutored child of that wilderness, on the one hand, and a child of the nascent frontier civilization, on the other hand. What was the measure of that civilization? It may even shock us a little to contemplate the civilization of much more modern times. *Pure civilization,* which will be the manifestation of universal obedience to God's law, has never existed. It will be remembered that imprisonment for debt was allowed by us, within the recollection of people who are still young: that the disabilities of the Jews have not been long removed in all parts of America and enlightened England, while there are parts of the world — not in heathendom — in which the Israelites are still locked up at night-fall, in the quarters of the cities they inhabit. We must recollect that the Florida war occurred within the last three decades; that Utah, with its tolerated abominations of Mormonism, is growing into a power under our eyes; and lastly, it is not "beyond the memory of man," that human slavery existed in the United States, and that doctors of divinity unfrocked themselves to fight in its defense. We are, therefore, not to pride ourselves conceitedly on the masculine civilization of our time, which affects to look disdainfully on Maryland and Massachusetts, whose statutes, in colonial days, offered bounties for Indian scalps.

Ninety years ago, the ideas and purposes of frontier-men were primitive and precautionary. It was an armed society of hunting agriculturists. Men ploughed the fields with their rifles slung over their shoulders. The Pioneer, axe in hand, wanted the land denuded of forest for cultivation. The Indian wanted the same land covered with forest, for his game. It was the direct conflict between enterprise getting bread by labor, and idleness getting food by luck. Of course, the Pioneer was the intrusive aggressor; the Indian, the conservative protector; the former, comparatively few in numbers, and forced to be prompt and wary; the latter numerous, and fearing not only the superior weapons of his foe, but the organization and discipline, which together made the comparatively few equal to the greater number. "What was called the frontier," says a writer who was familiar with the border life of America in the middle of the eighteenth century, " was constantly changing and diverging westwards, so that the habits and feelings of the people remained the same many miles eastward, after the frontier was changed.

Our frontier inhabitants were constantly exposed to a predatory war with the Indians, not embodied as an army publicly invading our country, but as a predatory banditti, attacking individuals and families, remote from a dense population. These attacks were often at night, or just at break of day; sometimes killing all the family, at others only a part, namely, the men and small children, leading the women and elder children captives, but, I believe, always burning the houses, and stealing the horses." In my own family, there are records of brutal outrages on its members in Western Virginia, in which the living were slaughtered while in the act of performing the rites of sepulture to their offspring in their forest homes, and even the dead were torn from the coffin, and hung on trees for the sake of the trophy scalp.

In truth, the natures as well as the purposes of the two antagonistic races that were constantly bordering on each other, were so completely inharmonious and irreconcilable, that the life of the resolute and exasperated Pioneer was concentrated on the impulse to get rid of Indians with as little compunction as if they had been vermin. Indeed, with many of the early adventurers, there was but little difference between a savage and a snake. The legislation of the time was also a picture of public necessity and opinion, while its bounties and rewards for scalps, were direct invitations to private warfare against what was called in the statutes, our "Indian enemies."

Such was the meager civilization of the frontier, when Cresap and Logan lived. On both sides, abstinence from revenge seems to have been considered dangerous timidity, or acknowledged fear. And so, Logan was a savage of his day, while Cresap's merit must rest on his personal history, as set forth herein, cleared entirely of the stain of wanton cruelty, and on his devotion to the cause of his country of which he was one of the earliest and bravest defenders. He died in its service, out-ranking several of the Marylanders, who afterwards became generals during the revolutionary war.

Baltimore, 1867.

INTRODUCTORY

If we look on the map at the portion of this continent occupied by us at present, we are amazed at the vast expansion of our territorial limits within much less than one hundred years. In the middle of the last century the British Dominions in America were but a fringe upon the Atlantic shores. Beginning in the Bay of Fundy their outline ran south-westward skirting the eastern shore of Lake Ontario until it touched the northern spurs of the Alleghenies, and then, descending along the slopes of those mountains, struck the northernmost angle of Florida, and finally terminated on the Atlantic at the mouth of the Altamaha. The average breadth of this scant region was not more than five degrees. West and north-west were the vast primeval forests, the gigantic lakes and rivers, claimed, by the French as Canada and the Province of Louisiana; while south, on the Gulf of Mexico and the Atlantic, stretched the romantic shores of Florida, under the dominion of Spain. It was not until the epoch of the Indian troubles, of which I am about to speak, and on the eve of our revolutionary war, that the Ohio became the recognized boundary between the white and the red man; and he who now entering one of those floating palaces of the western waters at Pittsburgh, descends the Ohio to the Mississippi, and the Mississippi to the Gulf, can hardly believe that within less than ninety years, the whole of this magnificent region, where the progress of trade has not effaced all traces of romantic nature, was still a dreary and dangerous wilderness, tenanted by wild beasts or by human beings almost as savage. There are men, still living who recollect the incidents of Indian warfare in Maryland, Pennsylvania, or Virginia, and can recount the escape, or the death of some ancestor by the tomahawk and scalping knife. There are those amongst us, too, whose hair is still un-silvered, who may remember their sport as boys in watching the straggling Indians,— half beggars, half bandits,—who every winter thronged our streets, but whose only use of the bow and the arrow was to win the pennies we ventured in order to test the sureness of their aim.

But where is the *far west,* which in those days was spoken of as something mysteriously indefinite, — as something denoting perils of journey and of Indian cruelty? It was then that we had still territorial boundaries to settle with Britain, and titles as well as rights to adjust with stubborn tribes. It was then that the far-seeing and comprehensive merchant laid the foundation of his wealth, by tracking the beaver in its wildest haunts in Oregon. It was then that California was remembered as a field of romantic missionary labor, cherished under Mexican viceroys, but as a land of abandoned enterprise. It was then that our young and restless spirits sought the valleys of the Ohio and Mississippi as homes which were beginning to be redeemed from the hunter and the savage. That was the far west of those days. But now, strange names salute our ears, sounding no more of Indian conquests, but commemorative monuments of victories over civilized men. We have abandoned an Indian nomenclature and adopted the calendar of Christian saints. Sante Fe, the Rio Bravo del Norte,— the Colorado of the West,— the Pecos,—the Gila, — the valleys of San Juan and Santa Clara, — the plains of the Sacramento and San Joaquin, and the upland Vale at the foot of Mount Shasta;— the Great Basin, around whose saline waters the Mormons have settled; — Monterey, — San Francisco, — San Diego, — Chrysopolae or the Golden Gates,— the lately ceded Russian territory,—and last of all, the Pacific, itself, for an acknowledged boundary, and the Isthmus for a highway. There is, no longer, a *far west.* States, now planting on the brink of the Pacific and washed by its surge, curb, in that direction, the utmost possible limit of our dominion. Gold, in apparently inexhaustible quantities, has magnetically attracted an immense population in the brief space of twenty years. The first great experiment of planting the Anglo-Saxon race on the Pacific, facing the Indies, with a clear and short highway in front, is no longer a problem to be solved. The tide of emigration sets no more exclusively from east to west, but rapidly ebbs and surges backward, as China, Hindustan, the Australian colonies, the Pacific islands, the Chilean, Peruvian, and Mexican states, pour their motley crowds of eager immigrants along the whole coast from the Gila to the Columbia. The icy tops of the Sierra Nevada are passed, and the great upland Basin of Utah becomes the thoroughfare of traders, pilgrims, and caravans from the Far East. Through the wilderness to Santa *Fe,* and thence along the southern passes of the mountains, other crowds press each other, to and fro, on the path of the modern Ophir. And thus, in the progress of a few brief years, the swollen tides of humanity, bursting the barriers of the Alleghenies from the east and of the Nevada from the west, must at last meet and mingle in the great valley of the Mississippi, which is destined to become the central mart of our mighty union.

In God's genial providence of gradually opening the resources of this world for the progress of mankind there is the most perfect accommodation to the enlarging wants and capacities of our race. Everything is not disclosed at once. The good, the desirable, the necessary, are hidden in the earth's secret places, and the task of laborious enterprise is imposed on man for their discovery and useful preparation. Yet, marvelous as are the modern developments of industry, of science, and, sometimes even, of apparent chance, there is no exhaustion in these resources, for new means of success seem to keep constant pace with each new labor and enterprise. Our beneficent Father works out his wonderful schemes by human agents not by miracles. Humanity, with all its virtues and all its sins, is charged with the noble task of free development, and thus the results become the work of man and are made the trials and tests of his responsibility.

The old world became crowded, and space was required in which the cramped and burdened millions might find room for industry and independence, — and a new continent was suddenly disclosed for their occupation. The old political systems of Europe and of the Eastern nations decayed in consequence of the encroachments of power made despotic by corruption or force, — and a virgin country was forthwith opened as a refuge for the oppressed masses, in which the principle of absolute political and religious freedom might be tried without any convulsive effort to cast off the fetters of feudalism. The labor of man, even in this new world, began to strip commercial countries of their forests, or made them too valuable for fuel,— and suddenly the heart of the earth is found to be veined with minerals which will save, for nobler purposes, the majestic woods that shade and shelter the surface. Coal thus becomes the most potent agent in commercial development, for, without it, the seas could not be traversed with the rapidity and certainty exacted by modern wants. The increasing industry and invention of the large populations of various countries, required, either a greater amount of capital to represent their productions, or a new standard of value for the precious metals already in circulation, — and, at once, apparently by mere accident, an adventurer discovered amid the rocks and rivers of the Pacific coast, a golden region in which the fabled sands of Pactolus are realized. At last, even steam itself becomes too slow for mankind, and human skill, chaining magnetism to its purposes and lacing the earth with its wires, embroiders the whole world with the electricity of thought. Soon, the railway will girdle the continent. But all these vast storehouses of invention, comfort and wealth, are not placed at our doors, in the midst of civilization, ready to be grasped, comprehended or used with equal ease by the dainty idler or the patient worker. Far away in distant regions they lie, amid forests and perils. Far away, in lands which are reached by tedious travel, requiring the renewal of hope in desponding hearts, and renewal of energy in broken men... There they repose, — long concealed and wisely garnered temptations, — to be discovered at the appropriate moment in the world's progress, and to lead man thither as the founder of new fields of human industry.

In this gradual development of the earth three classes of persons have always been needed: — the Discoverer, the Conqueror, and the Pioneer. Emigration is the overflowing of a bitter cup. Men do not leave their native lands and kindred for the perils of the wilderness, or for a country with which they have no community of laws, language, or present interest, unless poverty or bad government crowds them into the forest. When the Discoverer and the Conqueror have found the land and partly tamed the savage, the Pioneer advances into their field of relinquished enterprise, and his task partakes, in some degree, of the dangers incurred by both his predecessors. He is always a lover and seeker of independence, and generally pursues it with a laudable desire to improve his lot; yet the perfect exercise of this independence sometimes becomes selfishly exclusive. Its essence, in our country, is the complete self-reliance of the one man or the one family. This spirit of social, political, and industrial independence occasionally becomes wild, impatient and uncontrollable. Its mildest exhibition under such circumstances is in rude manners or wayward lawlessness, which outraged neighborhoods are wont summarily to redress. True civilized liberty does not countenance such mockers of justice within its pale, and thus there are multitudes who go voluntarily and wisely into new lands, while other heedless or worthless crowds are scourged by society into the forest. Slowly and surely are these elements of new states gathered, purged, and crystallized around the centers of modern civilization. Hope, ambition, misery, avarice, adventure, noble purpose, drive off impatient men who will not be satisfied with the slow accretions of wealth in the old communities. They require fortune and position by a leap. Independence demands space for the gigantic inspirations of its vast lungs, and flies headlong into the forest. The wandering woodsman or hunter gathers his brothers in armed masses for protection amid this chaos of unorganized freedom, and they support each other cheerfully in seasons of danger or disease. But the social law of humanity vindicates itself against the eager spirit of perfect independence. Wherever man who has once either drained or sipped the cup of civilization is found, there must he be fed and clothed, nor does he cease to yearn for the relinquished luxuries, amusements, or comforts of the home he abandoned beyond the eastern mountains. Wherever man goes, man's representative,—money,—pursues him; and secretly he longs for the pleasing results of that civilization which he feigns to despise. Thus the Pioneer may be said to bait the forest like a trap, for the Trader. Taking up the conflict with the Indian where the Conqueror left it, he at once subdues the soil and the savage. The Farmer, at length, plants himself on the land that the Hunter wrests from the Indian. The Merchant covers with his sails the seas that were scourged by the Pirate. The dollar dulls the edge of the bowie-knife. Where the Pioneer treads, the Missionary follows. Element by element, civilization drops in. Peace, like a cooling shadow, follows the blaze of war; and the law of God, vindicating by its ultimate success, the merit of peace, whose triumphs are the only true ones, plants the forest with cities, and that which was wildly won is quietly and permanently enjoyed.

Our habitual and perhaps almost necessary devotion to *the Present* in a country where property is so little treasured or transmitted in families, and our prying anxiety to know the secrets of the future, have made us too heedless of the memory of the Past. Our law of history, like our law of property, not only prevents an entail of our accumulations, but the Past and the Present may be said to disinherit the Future, or to leave few legacies. Yet I have ventured to hope that it would not be uninteresting to Marylanders, if I spoke to them of the days that are gone, and endeavored, by a glimpse of our " scant antiquity," to display the romantic story of some of our own people who were among the first in Lord Baltimore's province to mark the pioneer progress towards the west. Maryland thrust geographically as a wedge between the great provinces of Pennsylvania and Virginia was among the earliest to furnish her quota of stalwart foresters, who in their contests with the Indian prepared themselves for the subsequent conflict with England in the war of Independence.

It will be remembered that it was only a few years after Pontiac's war that small detachments of whites had crept westward through the defiles of the Alleghenies and along the principal paths, the northernmost of which converged at old Port Du Quesne or Pitt, whilst the southernmost led to the fountains of the Holston and the Clinch. A town was laid out on the east bank of the Monongahela within two hundred yards of Fort Pitt, and, for seventy miles above it, a route had been cut through the wilderness to Red-Stone Old Fort, near the mouth of Dunlop's Creek, now the site of Brownsville.

As late as 1774, Virginia still *claimed* by virtue of her charter, all the territory between the parallels of 36° 30' and 39° 40' north latitude, from the margin of the Atlantic due west the Mississippi, and thus enclosed within her assumed limit, not only the region which at present is comprised in Kentucky, but also the southern half of Illinois, one third of Ohio, and an extensive part of western Pennsylvania.* Settlements had been planted upon most of the eastern branches of the Monongahela, the Youghiogheny, and on the small eastern tributaries of the upper Ohio, for one hundred and twenty miles below Pittsburgh, as well as on the sources of the Greenbrier, the little Kanawha and Elk River, west of the mountains,—embracing in these districts, the north western counties of Virginia and the south western of Pennsylvania as at present defined. Pittsburgh was claimed as a frontier town of Virginia; while the southern settlements, on the tributaries of the Monongahela, were held *to* belong to the same province.

* It seems clear that by her new and enlarged charter of 1G09, the limits of Virginia were to extend "from Sea to Sea, west and North West."—1 *Land Laws of the U. S.,* p. 105. It is also clear that Great Britain did not, at the peace of 1763, lay claim to the French and Spanish settlements west of the Mississippi; nor, did our commissioners at the peace of Paris in 1783.

Yet the vast region south of the little Kanawha and westward thence to the Mississippi, with but slight exceptions, was a wilderness held by savages. The lonely, isolated settlements of a few poor, ignorant French colonists on the Wabash and Illinois Rivers, had, it is true, fallen under British dominion, after the peace of Paris, but these immigrants were scarcely regarded as British subjects, and were held as outlying foreign military colonists, many hundred miles in advance of civilization, having but little interest or sympathy with the pioneers who penetrated the wilderness from Virginia, Pennsylvania or Maryland.

The French and Indian wars and the true pioneer spirit which characterized so many Americans at that day had sprinkled this rough woodland region with enterprising traders, hunters, and agriculturists, and with brave women who were proper mates for men stamped with such energy and fortitude in the iron mintage of border trial. The majority of this class was hardy and virtuous, though, as in all frontier communities, the honest and daring were followed by miscreants willing either to shelter themselves from law in the wilderness, or to encounter the risks of a wild life without caring for ultimate results. The pioneer was a liberal and hospitable being, for he appreciated the loneliness and discomforts of his own perilous lot, and was prompt to ameliorate the condition of all who ventured beyond the Alleghenies. His fringed and fanciful hunting shirt, which may still be found among the mountains of our own Cumberland,—his deer-skin leggings,— his gaily embroidered moccasins—his tomahawk and scalping knife,— his bullet pouch, powder horn, and ready rifle,—made up his personal equipments of comfort and defense. He was a picturesque being as he was seen descending the slopes of the mountains or relieved against the blue sky or the dark shadows of the forest. In this lonely region no mechanics were to be hired, and every pioneer was obliged to do his own work or possess within his family the necessary laborers in the field or at the plough, the loom, and the anvil. His gun was in constant use against the Indian as well as the bear and the deer. Yet never was he an ungenerous neighbor when a new cabin was to be erected for an immigrant, or a crop to be gathered for the friend or stranger who inhabited his district. The "husking match" and the "log rolling" are distinctly recorded among the kindly memorials of early settlements in those days when the genuine *cabin,* made without nails, mortar or bricks, was the home of many an ancestry that has given rulers to our Union. A common danger cemented these forest settlements in a bond of mutual defense and interest. It was a life of incessant wariness or of peril to be encountered; and thus, mutual dependence and the fear of the savage, formed the best police of the pioneer, for it warned off weak and irresolute interlopers, and permitted none but the hardy and faithful to abide in the forest.

Nor were these men so improvident as to omit strengthening themselves, not only by acts of faith and friendship, but by supplying their bands with forts, block houses and stations, erected of massive logs and slabs, proof against bullets, and built around or near a never-failing spring. These defenses, constructed at points easy of access as places of refuge to a whole neighborhood of agriculturists or hunters, were perfect safe guards against a foe who had no artillery; yet, were rarely tenanted unless at periods of general alarm, or when the pioneers left their farms in the spring upon the announcement of some Indian murder in the vicinity.

These adopted children of the wilderness were, of course, not unskilled in wood craft. The stars, the sun, the bark of trees were their guides. The weather informed the settler whether he was to encounter his game for the day on the mountain tops, the hill sides or in the valleys ; and when the buck was slain, skinned, and dressed, the early night was passed in glee and story around the fire of his joyous hunting camp. Witchcraft was firmly believed by many of them; for strange sights and sounds, and a lonely life, gave play to the imagination or to the recollection of old superstitions learned in infancy. Singing, dancing, shooting the rifle, throwing the tomahawk, wrestling, and all athletic or manly sports, formed the constant diversions of the settlers when they were at leisure on holidays; while the most boisterous merriment prevailed at wedding frolics, or at the *housewarming* of the forest bride and her gallant groom. Lawyers were unknown in these rough and simple communities, yet a strong moral sense and the stern demands of necessity as well as of duty, preserved rights and interests in regions where no man could afford to be idle. Debts were seldom incurred. Laziness, dishonesty, and ill-fame roused the general public opinion of the settlement. Thieves were flogged. Personal disputes were settled by battles with fists, after which the parties became reconciled; and evil men, in the emphatic language of the day, were *hated out of the neighborhood.*

The wants of these backwoodsmen required an annual visit to the east, and every autumn associations were formed for the yearly caravan, which, with its long trains of horses, bearing peltries and Indian ware, might be heard tinkling its bells in the forests or along the mountain defiles as it wound its way to Hagerstown, Old Town, Cumberland and Baltimore, to exchange the products of the wilderness for salt, iron, lead and powder.*

* See Rev. Dr. Doddridge's *Notes on the Settlement and the Indian Wars of the Western Parts of Virginia and Pennsylvania,* from 1763 to 1783, Wellsburg, Va., 1824;—and Loudon's *Indian Wars,* Carlisle, Pa., 1808.

With these brief sketches of the land and inhabitants of that part of the North American wilderness which was most closely connected with Maryland just before the revolution, I shall proceed to delineate the deeds and career of some individuals whose names are linked with our state's story by romantic incidents which I believe have been and continue to be inaccurately recorded by American historians.

LOGAN AND CRESAP

The father of Captain Michael Cresap who has been portrayed as the instigator if not one of the chief actors in the alleged murder of the Indian Logan's family in the early part of 1774,— emigrated from Yorkshire, England, to America, when he was about fifteen years of age. We know nothing of his intervening career until fifteen years after, when he married a Miss Johnson, and settled either at or near Havre de Grace, on the Susquehanna. He was emphatically, a *poor man;* so poor, indeed, according to the family legends, that being involved in debt to the extent of nine pounds, currency, he was obliged soon after his inopportune marriage, to depart for the south in order to improve his fortune. He left his young wife in Maryland, and hastening to Virginia became acquainted with the Washington family, and rented from it a good farm, with the intention of removing finally to the flourishing colony. But on returning to Maryland he found that he had become a father, and that his resolute wife was loath to quit the Susquehanna for the Potomac. Accordingly, like a docile husband, he submitted to her whim, and contriving to free himself from debt, removed still higher up on the river to Wright's ferry, opposite the town of Columbia, where he obtained a Maryland title for five hundred acres of land. Unfortunately, however, for the settler, this was disputed ground, and as it was soon claimed under a Pennsylvania title a border war occurred, in which Cresap espoused the cause of Lord Baltimore with as much zeal as the Pennsylvanians sustained that of Penn. His enemies regarding him as a powerful foe seem to have resorted to the basest means to rid themselves of his presence. An Indian was hired to assassinate him in his own house; yet, won by his kindness and hospitality, the savage disclosed the plot and was pardoned for the meditated crime. At length, however, a regular battle took place between the factionists, and Cresap's party having wounded several of Penn's partisans gained the day and kept the field.

Nevertheless, the Pennsylvania warriors soon rallied their discomfited forces and besieged the fort in which the Marylander had entrenched himself. But the stalwart Cresap held out bravely against all comers, though he was singled as the special victim of the assailants. Nevertheless, in time, he deemed it advisable to seek aid from his neighbors; and as his eldest boy, Daniel was at this time, about ten years old, he dispatched the young forester in the night to obtain the required

17

succor. The frontier stripling, apt as he already was in the ways of the wilderness, could not, however, elude the vigilant besiegers, and being taken captive, endeavored to destroy the hostile clan while assembled around the fire, by casting therein its whole stock of powder which he found tied up in a handkerchief. Fortunately for the party, he was detected in time to escape the disastrous explosion.

If the young Cresap was unable to blow up his father's assailants, the elder was well nigh doomed to the fate his son had designed for the followers of Penn. The besiegers finding that they could not dislodge the stubborn Yorkshire man from his lair, determined to set fire to the roof and thus to *roast him out* of his fortress! No terms of capitulation were offered; and as Cresap disdained to ask his life at their hands, he rushed to the door, and wounding the sentinel, escaped to his boat. But here, surrounded by superior numbers, he was seized, overpowered, bound, and thrown into the skiff. Nevertheless, as his captors were conveying him across the Susquehanna in the dark, he contrived, notwithstanding his ligatures, to elbow one of the guard into the water. The Pennites, in the darkness, mistaking their companion for Cresap, beset him, forthwith, with oars and poles, nor was it until the lusty cries and rich brogue of the unfortunate Irishman undeceived them, that he was relieved from the beating and the bath. Passing through Columbia to Lancaster, Cresap was heavily manacled; but even then, lifting his arms as soon as the work was done, he smote the smith on the head with his ironed hands and leveled him to the ground. Nevertheless, he was effectually a prisoner and was borne off in triumph to Philadelphia, where the streets, doors and windows were thronged with spectators to see the *Maryland monster,* who taunted the crowd by exclaiming half in earnest half in derision : —" Why this is the finest city in the Province of *Maryland!"*

The Pennsylvanians at length became weary of their sturdy and audacious guest, yet he would not depart until released by order of the king, after suffering probably more than a year's confinement.* In the meantime, his family sought shelter in an Indian town on the Codorus, near York, where it was hospitably entertained until his return. Finding his old neighborhood too dangerous or disagreeable, he soon removed to a valuable farm at Antietam; and as it was a frontier post, in advance of white population, he built, over a beautiful spring, a stone house which was half dwelling and half fortress.

* See Jacob's *Life of Cresap,* p. 25. The most complete details of these border difficulties, will be found in the manuscripts and records preserved at Annapolis in the Maryland State library; in Rupp's *History of York County, Pa.,* p. 547 to 563; and in Hazard's *Register of Pennsylvania,* p. 200 *et seq.,* and p. 209 *et seq.* of the second volume; in a sketch of the boundary dispute and hostilities growing out of it from 1728 to 1737, betwixt Lord Baltimore and the Penns. Cresap was an ardent partisan of the Maryland proprietor, and acted with great vigor in defense of his own and his lord's rights or demands. See, also, Gordon's *Hist. Penna.,* 221. Gordon and Day are brief, while Proud is silent. Cresap was released in consequence of an order from the king in council commanding both parties to refrain from further violence, to drop all prosecutions, and to discharge their respective prisoners on bail."

He seems to have possessed the deserved confidence of some of the most respectable families of Maryland; for in this new settlement, he commenced trading, partly on a borrowed capital of £500 which he obtained from Mr. Dulany. But unluckily his venture of skins and furs, sent to England, was lost in a ship captured by the French, and he was thus compelled to begin the world anew for the third time. Yet his honest heart did not fail under renewed misfortunes. He offered his land, consisting of about 1,400 acres, to Dulany, in payment of his debt; and being thus stripped of nearly all his worldly possessions, he removed, about 1742 or 174.3, to a spot, in what is at present Alleghany County, Maryland, called Old-town, or as he pleased to name it — Skipton — after the place of his nativity in England, situated on the north fork, a few miles above the junction of the north and south branches of the Potomac.* Here at length he established his permanent home, and finally acquired by industry and perseverance a large landed estate in the neighborhood, on both sides of the river in Maryland and Virginia.

* See Colden's *History of the Five Nations,* pp. 3 and 84, edition 1755. See Philadelphia treaty of 1742 and Canassateego's speech at the Lancaster treaty, 1744.

About this epoch, he renewed his intimacy with Washington, who always reposed confidence in him; and being known as a bold and skillful woodsman, he was employed by the parties who in 1748 formed the celebrated Ohio Company. This association, among whose members we find Lawrence Washington and his brother Augustine, received from the British king a grant of five hundred thousand acres, to be taken chiefly on the south side of the Ohio, between the Monongahela and Kanawha Rivers, west of the Alleghanies.* The object of the enterprise was to settle land, and to carry on the Indian trade on a large scale. But the French, alarmed by this threatened advance of English pioneers, began immediately to extend a line of forts along the Mississippi and Ohio, passing through a vast extent of territory claimed by Great Britain. In spite of all opposition, the English grantees pursued their enterprise, and Col. Cresap's knowledge of the country and of pioneer life, was of great service to them in tracing the very first road through the windings of the Alleghenies. As one of their agents in that region, he employed an Indian, named Nemacolin, to mark the road by the well known trail of the tribes, and it is said he performed his duty so well, that the army pursued the same route when Braddock marched to the west to dislodge the French.** Colonel Cresap thus stationed on the extreme outposts of civilization, became an important pioneer in the early development of the west; nor did he cease, many years afterwards, to devote his mind and hopes to those fine regions in which he saw the future grandeur of his country. When he had attained the patriarchal age of ninety, he conceived and digested a plan to explore as far west as the Pacific, and nothing but his advanced years prevented the accomplishment of an enterprise which he cherished with the enthusiasm of an early borderer.

* *Washington's Writings,* vol II, appendix vi, pp. 478 and 479, and appendix vii.

** Three quarters of a mile south of Frostburg, Alleghany County, Maryland, in a belt of wood-land, and on or near the line of what is pointed out as *Braddock's road,* I saw, in October of 1858, a large, staunch old milestone, still in excellent condition, which is alleged, by the people of the neighborhood, to be a relic of ante-revolutionary times. It is to be hoped that it will be preserved as one of the few monuments of the olden-time remaining in that region. I copied the inscriptions on both sides of this stone:

On the front:	*On the rear:*
—	—
11 MILE	
To F: Cumberland	
29 M: To	Our
Cap: Smyth's	
Inn & Bridge Big	Country's Right
Crossings The best	
Road to Red Stone	We will defend.
Old Fort	
64 M.	

The grants to the English company not only caused the French to establish their line of forts, but, as is well known, resulted in a war which retarded the advance of civilization. The Indians were roused, and desolated the border. Cresap, at his extreme frontier settlement among the Alleghany Mountains, held a most dangerous post; but it was an eagle's nest, fit for a bold spirit, and he would not willingly desert it.

When hotly pressed by the savage foe he fought his way to Conococheague, and having placed his family in safety, did not remain an idle spectator while ruin threatened the infant settlements on the head waters of the Potomac. The country swarmed with the savage *guerrilleros* of those days, and the hardy woodsman, adopting the Indian fashion of the times, took the war path with his own band and children, and struck the foe on several occasions at the western foot of the Savage mountain, where his son Thomas fell by an Indian's ball, and at Negro mountain where a gigantic African, who belonged to his party, bequeathed his name in death to the towering cliffs. In these fights Michael Cresap obtained his first lessons in Indian warfare.

After these early border conflicts were over, although he was sometimes afterwards harassed by the savages, the veteran pioneer reposed at his homestead, respected and honored until quieter days. He was a man of vigorous mind and body, and although his early education had been neglected, there are testimonials of his skill both in composition, surveying, and even handwriting, in the possession of our Maryland Historical Society, which would do honor to a man of better birth and opportunities.* At the age of seventy he visited England; and, while in London was commissioned by Lord Baltimore to run the western line of Maryland, in order to ascertain which of the two branches of the Potomac was, in reality, the fountain head of the stream. His map of this survey is in the possession of the Maryland Historical Society, and, together with his report, has been used by our legislature in the boundary discussion with Virginia.**

* In the Gilmor MSS., *Maryland Papers,* vol. I, article No. 8, in (he possession of the Maryland Historical Society, is the following original letter from Colonel Cresap, in which we have an interesting account of one of the Indian raids in 1763. It is written in a firm and formal hand, and would do credit to one of much more clerkly reputation. The letter is thus addressed on the outside:

"On His Lordship's Service: —

To His Excellency Horatio Sharpe, *Enquire, in Annapolis.*

"To be forwarded by Express.) and endorsed :
" *From Col. Cresap, 15 July,* 1763."

"Old Town, July 15th, 1763.

"May it please your Excellency

"I take this opportunity in the height of Confusion to acquaint you with our unhappy and most wretched Situation at this time, being in Hourly Expectation of being massacred by our Barbarous and Inhumane Enemy the Indians, we having been three days successively attacked by them, Viz : the 13,14 and this Instant. On the 13th as 6 men were shocking some wheat in the field 5 Indians firing on them as they came to do it and others Running to their assistance;— on the 14th 5 Indians crept up to and fired on about 16 men who were sitting and walking under a Tree at the entrance of my Lane about 100 yards from my House, but on being fired at by the white men, who much wounded some of them, they Immediately Run off and were followed by the white men about a mile all which way was a great Quantity of Blood on the Ground. The white men got 3 of their Bundles, containing sundry Indian Implements and Goods. About 3 Hours after several guns were fired in the woods, on which a party went in Quest of them and found 3 Braves Killed by them. The Indians wounded one man at their first fire tho' but slightly. On this Instant as Mr. Saml. Wilder was going to a house of his about 300 yards Distant from mine with 4 men and several women, the Indians rushed on them from a rising Ground, but they perceving them coming, Run towards my House hollowing, which being heard by those at my house, they run to their assistance and met them and the Indians at the Entrance of my lane, on which the Indians Immdiately fired on them to the amount of 18 or Twenty and Killed Mr. Wilder ;— the party of white men Returned their fire and killed one of them dead on the Spot and wounded severall of the others as appeared by Considerable Quantity of Blood strewed on the Ground as they Run off, which they Immdiately did, and by their leaving behind them 3 Gunns, one pistole, and Sundry other Emplements of warr &c. &c.

"I have inclosed a List of the Desolate men. Women and Children who have fled to my house which is inclosed by a small stockade for safety, by which you'll see what a number of poor Souls, destitute of Every necessary of Life are here penned up and likely to be Butchered without immediate Relief and assistance, and can Expect none, unless from the province to which they Belong. I shall submit to your wiser Judgment the Best and most Effectual method for Such Relief and shall conclude with hoping we shall have it in time."

"I am Honorable Sir

Your Obedt. serv

THOS. CRESAP "

"P. S. those Indians who attacked us this day are part of that body which went southward by this way---- spring which is known by one of the gunns we got from them."

The Maryland Gazette of July 21, 1763, informs us that the colonel was not yet cut off by the savages, though it is feared he will be if not quickly relieved. The above story is repeated. Subsequent statements show that ten men were sent to assist Cresap.

**In the Gilmor MSS., *Maryland Papers*, vol. I, *Portfolio of "Surveys, letters, &c, connected with the rutting of the division line between Maryland and Pennsylvania,"* is the original autograph *map* made by Col. Cresap, in the neat style of a good country surveyor, and sent by him to Governor Sharpe. It came to Mr. Gilmor's possession with many other of the Ridout Papers, and is attested by Horatio Ridout, whose father was Sharpe's secretary. This was the *first* map ever made to show the course end fountains of the north and south branches of the Potomac River, in regard to which there has been so much controversy between Maryland and Virginia.

In 1770, after his return from England, George Washington visited Colonel Cresap at his Old Town settlement, in order to learn the particulars of the Walpole grant on the Ohio; and, as the future general of our armies returned from his examination of lands on the rivers of the west, he again tarried for the night in the humble dwelling of the old pioneer.* He had thus acquired the respect and confidence, not only of the Lord Proprietor of this Province, and of Washington, but was generally known in Maryland, Virginia, and Pennsylvania, as an energetic, far-seeing and hospitable man. No deed of needless daring or of cruelty is recorded against him; even the Indians who knew his rifle well, esteemed him cordially. When Nemacolin departed for the mountains of Cumberland, he left his son in Cresap's care. The savages with whom he had dealt so fiercely when necessity demanded, as they went, during his latter years, past his house on their hunting expeditions, were always welcomed and entertained. He had a huge ladle, and kettle prepared expressly to feast them with a whole ox, and they, in turn complimented his hospitality by bestowing on him the Indian title of the Big Spoon.**

* *Washington's Writings,* vol II, pp. 516 and 533. *Journal of Tour to the Ohio River.*

** Jacob's *Life of Capt. Michael Cresap.* Cumberland, Md., 1828. The Rev. John J. Jacob, by whom this biographical sketch of the life of Captain Michael Cresap was written, entered the store and was engaged in the western trading concerns of Captain Cresap, from the age of fifteen. This was about the year 1772. He was entrusted with the management and settlement of valuable ventures sent by the captain to Redstone Old Fort, or Brownsville, during the Indian war of 1774. When the revolutionary conflict broke out, and after Cresap's death on the 18th of October, 1775, Jacob remained for a while with the hero's family; but, in July, 1776, he entered the militia as an ensign, and subsequently obtained a lieutenant's commission in the regular army with which he continued during five campaigns, until the winter of 1781. In this year he married the widow of Capt. Michael Cresap, his old employer: and thus, becoming possessed of all his papers, and being intimate with his motives and history during a close personal intercourse, he was fully enabled as well as entitled, to vindicate the memory of his departed friend

Later in life he was known as an esteemed clergyman of the Methodist Episcopal church, who, for many years, resided and finally died, as a local minister in Hampshire County, Virginia.

Since the first publication of this narrative, Mr. John J. Jacob, of Romney, Virginia, has informed me by letter, dated July 16, 1851, that his father did not leave the army as a lieutenant but as captain. He adds: "It is a small matter, but as " he won his way by his sword and integrity, let justice be done to his memory; and I know the old 6th Regt., Maryland Line, would heartily assert his claim."—*MS. Letter.* On the original rolls of the members of the Cincinnati Society of Maryland, deposited with the Maryland Historical Society, John J. Jacob is entered as a *Lieutenant,* from Washington County, Md., who resigned in January, 1781, after four years and three months service.

At the age of eighty he married a second time. He visited the British possessions, near Nova Scotia, at one hundred, and died at the age of one hundred and six! Such was the father of Captain Michael Cresap whose name has been doomed most unjustly to disgrace, as that of a murderer, by Mr. Jefferson's adoption of the falsehood contained in a miscalled Indian speech.

Michael, the youngest son of the pioneer, whose biography I have sketched, was born in a part of Frederick which is now comprised in Alleghany County in this state, on the 29th June, 1742. In those early days there were no seminaries of learning in that remote region; and Michael was sent to a school in Baltimore County, under the charge of Rev. Mr. Craddock. A wild mountain boy from the wilderness, he had, at first, but few friends among the eastern pupils; yet, with the usual success of courage and generosity he soon fought his way into the good graces of his schoolmates. But the restraints of school life were uncongenial to his habits, and flying from his preceptor, he traversed alone the one hundred and forty miles between Mr. Craddock's and his home. The old colonel, however, did not sanction the conduct of the truant, but, believing in the virtue of the rod, and the necessity of filial obedience as well as of education, flogged him severely, and sent him back to his teacher, with whom he steadily remained until his studies were finished.

Soon after leaving school, he married a Miss Whitehead, of Philadelphia, and the young pair, almost children, departed to the mountains to enjoy, as the romantic striplings probably supposed, love in a cottage in a little frontier village near his father's dwelling among the hills. But the colonel would not countenance a life of idleness, and at once established Michael as a trader. Trade, in those days and neighborhoods, was often a perilous business in the hands of inexperienced men; and young Cresap, who imported largely from London, and dealt with the utmost liberality, so often found his confidence misplaced, that in the course of a few years he was nearly ruined. Notwithstanding his kindness and honorable deportment, he seems to have had enemies, or at least extremely suspicious watchers of his acts. The agent of the London merchant, from whom he received his goods in America, reported to his principal in England, that Michael was a doubtful character, and might probably remove to some parts of the western wilds where he would be out of the reach of the law. The consequence of this report was the immediate withdrawal of the young trader's customary supplies; but, as soon as Michael was able to trace the slander to its source, he charged it directly upon the London agent, and the controversy ended in a violent personal conflict in a private room in Fredericktown.

Cresap was thus compelled, both by the blow which his credit had received and his bitter experience among his customers, to curtail his business. Yet hope did not desert him. The population which had gathered around this frontier settlement began, under the temptations of the west, to flow off towards the Ohio. His active temper and promptness soon decided him. Urged by necessity as well as by a laudable ambition, and allured by the rational and exhilarating prospect before him, he saw or though the saw, in the rich bottoms of the Ohio, an ample fund, if he succeeded in obtaining a title to those lands, not only to redeem his credit and extricate him from difficulty, but to afford a respectable competency for his rising family.

"Under this impression, and with every rational prospect of success, early in the year 1774, he engaged six or seven active young men at the rate of £2 10s. per month, and repairing to the wilderness of the Ohio, commenced the business of building houses and clearing lands; and, being among the first adventurers into this exposed and dangerous region, he was enabled to select some of the best and richest of the Ohio levels." *

* Jacob's *Life of Cresap*, p. 49.

After the Indian and French wars and the treaty made by Bouquet, the attention of Maryland, Virginia, and Pennsylvania settlers, had been attracted to the great trans-Alleghany region watered by the Monongahela, the Ohio, Kanawha, the Scioto, the Cheat and their affluents. Companies had been formed and lands granted. The outposts, the scouts and pickets of civilization, were fixed along the streams. Fort Du Quesne had become Port Pitt, under the British flag. Wheeling was a station; and, all along the river, there were spots where traders and farmers had settled, or neighborhoods gathered for mutual protection around blockhouses, forts and stockades. In this society, laudably engaged in repairing his fortune and preparing for that of his young family, I shall leave Michael Cresap early in the year 1774, and carry you for a short time to another and perhaps more romantic scene among the hills and valleys of the Susquehanna.

Indian history and especially Indian biography must always resemble the pictorial sketches of the Indians themselves, who, by a few rude etchings on a rock, a few bold dashes on the skin of a buffalo or scratches on the bark of a birch tree, record the outlines which may serve to recall an event, though they can only commemorate a character by inferences. Their story is but a skeleton; and hard, indeed, is the task which attempts to clothe the dry and dusty bones with flesh, or to make the restored being move with at least the semblance of real life. Their theatre is the forest; their home a camp; their only architecture a cabin or a perishable tent; their only permanent and consecrated resting place the grave! A solitary and dangerous people, almost without a record, they flit like shadows through the wilderness of wood, prairie and mountain ; now here, now gone in the dim recesses of the valleys; free as the deer, or transient as phantoms of mingled romance and horror; but generally inscribing their wild, red marks in the memory of white men by deeds of cruelty and blood alone.

In the early days of Pennsylvania the valley of the Susquehanna was assigned by the Six Nations as a hunting ground for the Shawanese, Conoys, Nanticokes, Monseys, and Mohicans; and Shikellamy, or as he was called by the Moravians, Shikellemus, a chief sent by those nations to preside over a tribe, dwelt at Shamokin,* an Indian village of about fifty houses and nearly three hundred persons, built on the broad level banks of the Susquehanna, on a beautiful site, with high ranges of hills both above and below it, affording magnificent views of the picturesque valley in whose lap the modern Sunbury is quietly nestled. This Shikellamy, the father of Logan, is alleged by Bartram to have been a "Frenchman born in Montreal, Canada, but adopted by the Oneidas after being taken prisoner. **

* Compare *Minutes of Council* Aug. 12, 1731, Brainerd's *Journal,* and *Loskiel,* part 2d, p. 119. Speaking of his visit to Shamokin, Brainerd says. "about one half of its inhabitants are Delawares, the others called Senecas and Tutelas." *Loskiel,* part 2d, p. 119, speaks of Shikellemus as "the first magistrate and head chief of all the Iroquois Indians on the banks of the Susquehanna as far as Onondaga." And in the same work, part 2d, p. 91: "Shamokin" is called, "a town belonging to the Iroquois." At the treaty of 1742, Shikellemus was present, but what tribe or place he represented is not stated; there were also in attendance, several "Delawares of Shamokin." Gordon, *History Pennsylvania,* p. 250, alludes to the Delawares of Shamokin. In 1744, Conrad Weiser was sent to Shamokin to inquire into the murder of John Armstrong, an Indian trader and his two servants, Woodworth Arnold and James Smith, alleged to have been committed by some of the Shamokin band of Delawares. He delivered his message "to the Delaware chief Allumpoppies and the rest of the Delaware Indians, in the presence of Shikellamy and a few more of the Six Nations."—Rupp's *History of Northumberland, Huntington, Mifflin, etc., etc., Counties, Pennsylvania,* p. 86.

It is probable that Shikellamy presided over the Iroquois, only, who settled at Shamokin, and, perhaps, over the Tutelas, who seem to have been incorporated into the Six Nations. Gallatin's *Synopsis, Trans. Am. Antq. Soc,* vol. II, pp. 75, 81. *Draper MSS.*

When Count Zinzendorf, on the 28th of September, 1742, accompanied by Conrad Weiser, two Indians, brother Mack and his missionary wife, after a tedious transit through the wilderness on their journey of Christian love, entered this beautiful vale of Shamokin, Shikellamy was the first to step forth to welcome them, and, after the exchange of presents, to promise his aid as a chief in fostering the religion of Christ among the tribe. But when David Brainerd visited the Indian village, three years after, he found that the seed dropped by the Moravians had fallen on barren places. He was kindly received and entertained by the Indians, yet neither his request nor the illness of one of the tribe could induce them to forego their wild and noisy revels. "Alas," exclaims the journalist, "how destitute of natural affection are these poor uncultivated pagans, although they seem kind in their own way! Of a truth, the dark corners of the earth are full of the habitations of cruelty. The Indians of this place are accounted the most drunken, mischievous, and ruffian-like fellows in these parts; and Satan seems to have his seat in this town in an eminent manner"

** There is some curious information in my possession in regard to the nativity of this *Shikellamy*, the father of Logan, showing that he was a Frenchman from Montreal, and consequently that the famous Logan was not a full blooded Indian. It is found in an excessively rare tract, entitled " *Observations on the Inhabitants, Climate, Soil, Rivers, Productions, Animals, and other Matters worthy of Notice, made by John Bartram, in his Travels from Pennsylvania to Onondaga, Oswego and the Lake Ontario in Canada, to which is annex'd a curious Account of the Cataracts of Niagara by Peter Kalm, a, Swedish Gentleman who traveled there,* London 1751." In this journey Bartram was accompanied by Lewis Evans, the geographer; Conrad Weiser, the Indian interpreter; and, *from Shamokin,* by Shikellamy. "July 10, 1743 : we departed in the morning with Shikellamy and his son, he being the chief man of the town which consisted of Delaware Indians; he was of the Six Nations, *or rather a Frenchman born at Montreal, and adopted by the Oneidas after being taken prisoner;* but his son told me *he* was of the *Cayuga* nation — that of his mother — agreeable to the Indian rule, *partus sequitur ventrem,* which is as reasonable among them as among cattle, since the whole burden of bringing up falls on her; therefore in case of separation the children fall to her share."— *Observations, S.c,* p. 17.

The Six Nations used Shamokin as a convenient tarrying place for their war parties against the southern Catawbas; and, soon after the missionaries visited them, they were desirous to have a blacksmith from the white settlements, who would reside permanently in their village, and save their long journeys from the mountains to Tulpehocken or Philadelphia. The governor of the province allowed the request, provided the smith should continue only as long as the Indians remained friendly to the English; and the Moravians, availing themselves of the opportunity, dispatched a staunch brother named Anthony Schmidt, from their mission at Bethlehem, who, doubtless, in the intervals of his business of repairing the savages' rifles, was enabled, as an antidote, to edify them with a sermon on the horrors of war. The blacksmith, however, opened the way for the establishment of a Moravian mission at Shamokin in 1747, under the charge of Brother Mack. Bishop Camerhoff and the pious Ziesberger visited it in 1748; and, in the following year, Shikellamy—this apparently virtuous chief over so boisterous, drunken and roistering a tribe—a man who is reported to have performed many embassies between the government of Pennsylvania and the Six Nations, as well as attended important councils at Philadelphia — departed for the Indian hunting grounds which lie in the pleasant prairies of the spirit land beyond the grave.*

*Conrad Weiser, an officer in the Indian Department of Pennsylvania, and the Moravians seems to have had great confidence in Shikellamy, who probably died a sincere friend of the whites. For an account of his death and character, see Day's *Penn. Hist. Coll.,* p. 526. *Loskiel.* Rev. J. Heckewelder's statement, appendix No. iv to Jefferson's *Notes on Virginia.*

Unto this personage, thus reared in a sort of fear, love, or admiration of the whites, but in the midst of excessively bad associates—as described by Brainerd—was born a second son, celebrated in the annals of our country by the spicy rhetoric of a speech which first attracted the attention of Mr. Jefferson, and has since been repeated by every American school boy as a specimen of Indian eloquence and Indian wrongs.

After Braddock's defeat in 1755, the whole wilderness from the Juniata to Shamokin, and from the Ohio to Baltimore Town, was filled with hostile Indian parties—murdering, scalping, burning and destroying. I have not time to notice the breaking up of the mission at Shamokin and the slaughter of inoffensive whites throughout the neighborhood, in which all those miscalled friendly tribes were concerned as soon as they were encouraged by the successes of the French and the disasters of the English. Their former professed Christianity, or the forbearance of their chiefs, had, in all likelihood, been the effect of sudden superstition or salutary fear.*

* *Voyages dans la Haute Pennsylvanie,* tome III, chap. iv.

During this epoch the son of Shikellamy — Logan — who had been named it is said for the secretary of the province, whom his father knew and loved,* disappears from the scene. We have few historical or biographical anecdotes of his early life, nor does he in fact become the subject even of a legend until seventeen or eighteen years after his father's death.**

** Some early notices of the sons of Shikellamy and their deeds may be found in the following writers : Rupp's *History of Dauphin, Cumberland. Franklin, dec, Counties, Pa.,* pp. 65, 319, 84, 259, 100, 316. Also Rupp's *History of Northumberland County,* pp. 92,119, 166. Rupp's *History of Berks and Lebanon Counties, Pa.,* pp. 213, 41, 39, Rupp's *History of Northampton, Lehigh, &c, Counties, Pa.,* p. 103. Kercheval's *Valley of Va.,* p. 127. Loudon's *Narratives of Indian Wars,* vol. II, p. 233 ; this passage describes Logan's personal appearance in 1765, and recounts an anecdote or two.

The Juniata breaking through the wild gap of Jack's mountain, enters the southwestern end of Mifflin County, Pennsylvania, and meandering through Lewistown valley, again strikes the mountains at the romantic gorge of the Long Narrows, between the Black Log and Shade mountains, at a cleft barely wide enough for the river to pass, and, at its end, the stream bursts through the rocky masses of Shade Mountain. Kishicoquillas Creek is a never failing flood in this romantic neighborhood, fed by the mountain springs surrounding a valley out of which it leaps at a deep ravine in Jack's mountain, and enters the Juniata at Lewistown. Early settlements had been made in this attractive region, but when the Indian troubles broke out, the inhabitants fled, nor was it until the years between 1765 and 1769, that they began to return, and about that period, Judge Brown, Samuel Milliken, McNitt, James Reed and Samuel McClay, became the earliest dwellers in the charming valley of Kishicoquillas.

About a mile or two above the deep and tangled dell where the stream passes Jack's mountain, beside a beautiful limestone spring, at a spot which was as solitary as it was romantic, an Indian cabin had been built for many years. As William Brown and James Reed, two of the pioneers whom I have named as early occupants of this region, had wandered one day out of the valley in search of springs and choice locations, they suddenly started a bear, and, like all foresters, being provided with rifles, they immediately gave chase. A shot speedily wounded the beast, which retreating to the higher ground led them onward in quest of their prey, until suddenly this beautiful spring, gushing from the hill-side, burst upon their sight. Exhausted by a long and tedious hunt, the woodsmen were more delighted to find the stream than the game, and immediately resting their rifles against trees, threw themselves on the ground to drink. But as Brown bent over the clear mirror of the water, he beheld, on the opposite side, reflected in the limpid basin, the shadow of a stately Indian. With instinctive energy he sprang to regain his weapon, while the Indian yelled, whether for peace or war he was unable to determine; but as he seized his rifle and faced the foe, the savage dashed open the pan of his gun, and scattering the powder, extended his open palm in token of friendship. Both weapons were instantly grounded, and the men who a moment before had looked on each other with distrust, shook hands and refreshed themselves from the brook. For a week they continued together examining lands, seeking springs, and cementing a friendship which had been so strangely commenced at a period when "whoever saw an Indian saw an enemy, and the only questions that were asked, on either side, were from the muzzles of their rifles."

The Indian apparition of the spring was Logan, the son of Shikellamy, a solitary Indian; no chief, but a wanderer sojourning for a while on his way to the west.*

 * Day's *Hist. Coll. of Perm.*, p. 464, *et. seq. Pittsburgh Daily American*, 1842. *American Pioneer*, vol. I, p. 188.

Logan is well remembered and favorably described in the legends of this valley, for he was often visited in his camp by the whites. Upon one occasion, when met by Mr. McClay at the spring which is even now known by his name, a match was made between the white and red man to shoot at a mark for a dollar a shot.* In the encounter, Logan lost four or five rounds, and acknowledged himself beaten. When the whites were leaving the dell, the Indian went to his cabin, and bringing as many deer skins as he had lost dollars, handed them to Mr. McClay, who refused the peltries, alleging that he and his friends had been Logan's guests, and would not rob him, for the match had been merely a friendly contest of skill and nerve. But the courteous waiver would not satisfy the savage. He drew himself up with great dignity, and said in broken English: "Me bet to make you shoot your best; me gentleman, and me take your dollars if me beat!" So McClay was obliged to take the skins or affront his friend, whose sense of honorable dealing would not allow him to receive even a horn of powder in return.**

 * Day's *Coll., ut supra,* p. 46G, for a description of the site of this spring.
 ** Letter of 11. P. McClay in *Pittsburgh. Daily American* of 1842, and in *Perm. Ilist. Colt,* by Day, p. 467. *American Pioneer*, pp. i, 114,115, 188. At a mature period of his life, Logan was described as a very fine looking man: "He was a remarkably tall man and *considerably above six feet high,* strong and well proportioned; of a brave, open, manly countenance, and, to appearance, would not be afraid to meet any man." See Loudon's *Indian Narratives*, vol. II. p. 223, *et seq.,* for this description and some interesting anecdotes of him.

Deer hunting, dressing the skins and selling them to the whites, seem to have been the chief employments of Logan at this period, and the means of his livelihood. Upon one occasion he had sold a quantity to a tailor named De Yong, who dwelt in Ferguson's valley below the gap. Buckskin small clothes were in those days in demand among the frontier men as well as among the soldiers and the forts, and when silver or paper money was scarce, barter was the customary mode of trade in those simple communities. Logan, according to agreement, received his pay from the tailor in wheat, which, when taken to the mill, was found so worthless that the miller refused to grind it; but law and the ministers of justice, had already found their way into the secluded valley, and the Indian appealed to his friend Brown, who by this time had been honored with the commission of a magistrate. When the judge questioned him as to the character of the fraudulent grain, Logan sought in vain to find words to express the precise character of the material with which it was adulterated, but said it resembled the wheat itself. "It must have been *cheat*" said the judge. "Yoh!" exclaimed the Indian, "that's very good name for him! " and forthwith a decision was given in Logan's favor and a writ presented for the constable, which, he was told, would produce the money for his buckskins. But the untutored Indian, too uncivilized to be dishonest, could not comprehend by what magic this fragment of paper would force the reluctant tailor, against his will, to pay for the skins. The judge took down his commission emblazoned with the royal arms, and explained the first principles and operations of civil law, after which Logan appeared to be better satisfied with the gentle operation of judicial process, and departed to try its effect in his own behalf, exclaiming, "law *very* good if it make rogues pay!"

When one of Judge Brown's daughters was just beginning to walk, her mother expressed sorrow that she could not obtain a pair of shoes to give more firmness to her infant steps. Logan stood by but said nothing. Soon after he asked Mrs. Brown to allow the little girl to spend the day at his cabin near the spring. The cautious heart of the mother was somewhat alarmed by the proposal, yet she had learned to repose confidence in the Indian, and trusting in the delicacy of his feelings, assented to the proposal with apparent cheerfulness. The day wore slowly away, and it was near night when her little one had not returned. But just as the sun was setting the trusty savage was seen descending the path with his charge, and in a moment more the little one was in its mother's arms, proudly exhibiting on her tiny feet a pair of beautiful moccasins, the product of Logan's skill.*

* Narrative of Mrs. Norris, in Day's *Perm. Hist. Coll,* p. 467.

I have dwelt, perhaps tediously, upon these simple incidents of Indian and frontier life, because they are the only ones I have been able to glean from the brief records of Logan's career, that exhibit him to posterity in a favorable light. His lot was soon to be changed. The lonely, simple, untutored savage was shortly to come in violent conflict with the whites, who were "extending the area of freedom;" and the rest of his life was checkered with horrible crimes and maudlin regrets, dark enough to blur the gentle deeds of his early years. According to the statement of Judge Brown, Logan departed to the far-west soon after the occurrences I have recounted, and he never saw him more; but, in the language of the cordial old pioneer, "he was the best specimen of humanity, white or red, he ever encountered."

For a while, again, the curtain drops on our Indian legend, and the savage disappears behind the leaves of the forest,; nor do we find his trail again until the Rev. Mr. Heckewelder, when living as a missionary at the Moravian town on the Beaver, about the year 1772, four or five years after the events we have just narrated, was introduced by an Indian of that neighborhood to Logan as the son of old Shikellamy, the friend of the white men and Moravians at Shamokin. The savage impressed the missionary as a person of talents superior to Indians generally. He exclaimed against the whites for the introduction of spirituous liquors among his people; spoke of *gentlemen* and their true character, regretting that the tribes had unfortunately so few of this class for neighbors; declared his intention to settle on the Ohio below Big Beaver, where he might live in peace forever with the white men, but confessed to the missionary his unfortunate fondness for the fire-water. At that time Logan was encamped at the mouth of Beaver, and in 1773, when Heckewelder was journeying down the Ohio towards Muskingum, he visited the Indian's settlement and received every civility he could expect from the members of his family who were at home.*

* Appendix No. iv to Jefferson's *Notes on Virginia,* p. 46. J Wheelock's *Narrative,* 1772-73, p. 50.

It was about this time that another missionary, the Bev. Dr. David McClure, during a visit to Fort Pitt and the neighboring regions of the

Ohio, met our hero, and saw many other Indians who were in the habit of resorting to the settlements for the sake of a drunken frolic, staggering about the town. At that time Logan was still remarkable for the grandeur of his personal appearance. Tai-gah-jute,* or Short Dress, for such was his Indian name, stood several inches more than six feet in height; he was straight as an arrow; lithe, athletic, and symmetrical in figure ; firm, resolute, and commanding in feature; but the brave, open, and manly countenance he possessed in his earlier years was now changed for one of savage ferocity.** After tarrying and preaching nearly three weeks at Fort Pitt, Dr. McClure, in the summer or autumn of 1772, set out for Muskingum, accompanied by a Christian Indian as his interpreter. The second day after his departure, the way-farers unexpectedly encountered Logan. Painted, equipped for war, and accompanied by another savage, he lurked a few rods from the path beneath a tree, leaning on his rifle; nor did the missionary notice him until apprised by the interpreter that Logan desired to speak with him. McClure immediately rode to the spot where the red man stood, and asked what he wished. For a moment Logan remained pale and agitated before the preacher, and then pointing to his breast, exclaimed: "I feel bad here. Wherever I go the evil Manethoes pursue me. If I go into my cabin, my cabin is full of devils. If I go into the woods, the trees and the air are full of devils. They haunt me by day and by night. They seem to want to catch me, and throw me into a deep pit, full of fire!" In this strain of abrupt, maudlin musing, with the unnatural pallor still pervading his skin, he leant a while on his rifle, and continued to brood over the haunting devils. At length he broke forth with an earnest appeal to the missionary as to what he should do? Dr. McClure gave him sensible and friendly advice; counseled him to reflect on his past life; considered him as weighed down by remorse for the errors or cruelties of past years, and exhorted him to that sincere penitence and prayer which would drive from him the evil Manethoes forever.***

* "The aged Seneca, Captain Decker, told me that Logan's Indian name was Tah-gah-jute, or Short Dress, and added that 'he was a very bad Indian." — *Lyman C. Draper,* in a letter to Brantz Mayer.

** Compare Loudon's *Nar. Indian Wars,* vol. II, p. 223, and McClure and Parish's *Memoirs of Rev. Eleazar Wheelock,* Newburyport, 1811, p. 139. Loudon describes him about 1765, McClure in 1772. His intemperate habits had begun before the occurrence of the Yellow Creek tragedy in 1774, and, in 1772, he was already painted and equipped for war.

*** Wheelock's *Memoirs, ut ante,* p. 139, &c. I am indebted for this reference and anecdote to my friend Lyman C. Draper, who has kindly furnished it to me in MS.

The clergyman departed on his mission, nor did he ever hear of the Indian again until after the bloody deeds which will be hereafter recounted. The fire-water of the white men had begun to do its deadly work upon all the elements of a noble character in this untutored savage.

I must again shift the scenery of our stage and return once more to our Maryland settler, who had gone out with his band to the Ohio, early in the spring of 1774, although it is unquestionable that he had previously visited that region for the purpose of trading and locating land.

On an elevated and commanding bank on the east side of the Monongahela, about seventy miles above Pittsburgh, there were at that period the remains of one of those ancient works, which, in consequence of the military skill displayed in the selection of their site and arrangement of their walls or parapets, have been regarded as Indian forts. They are among the evidences of the supposed civilization of the races who inhabited the western valleys anterior to the present tribes, and of whom even the legends are lost. On the northwest of the one at present under consideration, the River Monongahela rushed along the base of the hill; on the northeast and south were deep ravines, while, on the east, a flat was spread out across which an approach could easily be detected. Several acres were enclosed within the works, and hard by were springs of excellent water.

This is the site of the town of Brownsville, the head of the steam navigation of the Mississippi valley, nearest the eastern mountains, and the spot, even at that early day, to which the main trail over the Alleghenies was directed. It became an attractive place to the whites as it had evidently been to the savages, as we may judge from the ingenious works with which they fortified it. This post, known in border history as Red-Stone Old Fort, became the rallying point of the pioneers and was familiar to many an early settler as his place of embarkation for the "dark and bloody ground." In the legends of the west, Michael Cresap, whom we left to sketch the biography of Logan, is connected with this Indian stronghold. In those narratives Cresap is spoken of as remarkable for his brave, adventurous disposition, and awarded credit for often rescuing the whites by a timely notice of the savages' approach, a knowledge of which he obtained by unceasing vigilance over their movements. This fort was frequently Cresap's rendezvous as a trader, and thither he resorted with his people, either to interchange views and adopt plans for future action or for repose in quieter times when the red men were lulled into inaction, and the tomahawk was temporarily buried. These were periods of great conviviality. The days were spent in athletic exercises, and, in the evening, the sturdy foresters, bivouacked around a fire of huge logs, recounted their hair-breadth adventures, or if, perchance, a violin or jews-harp was possessed by the foresters, it was certainly introduced, and the monotony of the camp broken by a boisterous *stag-dance.*

Michael Cresap discovered at that early day that this location would become exceedingly valuable as emigrants flowed in and the country was gradually opened. Accordingly, he took measures to secure a Virginia title to several hundred acres, embracing the fortification, by what, at that time, was called a *tomahawk improvement.* Not content, however, with girdling a few trees and blazing others, he determined to ensure his purpose; and, in order that his act and intention might not be misconstrued, he built a house of *hewed logs* with a shingle-roof *nailed* on, which is believed to have been the first edifice of this kind in that part of our great domain west of the mountains. We are not possessed of data to fix the precise year of this erection, but it is supposed to have occurred about 1770. The title to the property was retained in Cresap's family for many years, but was finally disposed of to the brothers Thomas and Basil Brown, who emigrated from Maryland.*

* MS. of James L. Bowman, published in the *American Pioneer* in 1843, and subsequently reprinted in Day's *Perm. Hist. Coll.,* p. 341, *et seq.*

We now approach the final scene of our sketch in the valley of the Ohio. Cresap in his last expedition to the west, had departed from Maryland, as I have already related, early in 1774, in order to open farms on the river, and was accompanied by hired laborers. But an Indian war was soon to break out which, in the history of the west, is sometimes known by the name of this Marylander, as Cresap's war, and sometimes by that of the earl of Dunmore, who was then governor of Virginia. Yet this savage conflict, in which the earl commanded the Virginians, and Cornstalk, a Shawanese chief, led the Indians, had probably a very different origin from that which we shall hereafter see was erroneously ascribed to it, and in which Michael Cresap was unjustly supposed to have acted so bloody a part.

During the ten years subsequent to the treaty made by Bouquet, the gradual advance of the whites to the west had been a constant source of alarm to the Indians. There was no acknowledged boundary between the races. Every year confused and confounded them more and more. Collisions and violent disputes were the natural and necessary results. Crimination and recrimination followed. The white men introduced his fire-water, and the Indian learned to love its wild delirium, nor did he regret the mad revels, and even the murders in which he participated while under its influence. The savage and the settler constantly encountered each other with mutual distrust. The town and the farm were to rise and spread out over the war path and hunting ground. The slow, eager, resistless encroachments of civilization, brought the two uncongenial and incongruous races, face to face, in contact, and the slightest breath was sufficient to fan into conflagration the fire that smoldered in the hearts of each.

Besides this, there had been no scrupulous fulfillment of Bouquet's treaty on the part of the Indians; and I am informed by one of our ablest border historians and scholars, that in these ten years of nominal peace, but in truth, of *quasi* war, more lives were sacrificed along the western frontiers than during the whole outbreak of 1774, including the battle of Point Pleasant.*

* MS. letter from Lyman C. Draper.

In order that I may not be supposed to allege these Indian exasperations carelessly, I will state, as I believe it to be unquestionable history that the Shawanese, failing to comply with the treaty of 1764, did not deliver their white captives, and barely acquiesced sullenly in some articles of compact, by command of the Six Nations. The Red-Hawk, a Shawanese insulted Colonel Bouquet with impunity, and an Indian killed the colonel's servant on the next day after peace was made. This wanton murder being disregarded at the time, gave rise immediately to several outrages.

In the following year individuals were slain by the savages on New River, and soon after, some men employed in the service of Wharton's company were waylaid and killed on their journey to Illinois, while their goods were plundered and borne *off* by the robbers. Sometime after this outrage, a number of men employed in slaughtering cattle for Fort Chartres, were slain, and their rifles, blankets and accoutrements carried to the Indian villages. All these brutal wrongs were un-redressed, and although the Shawanese are not supposed to have been the only perpetrators of the bloody cruelties, yet, unresisting submission to such enormities seems to have been a mistaken policy in an age in which the law of revenge, or of prompt, compulsory obedience was the only code comprehended by the savages. Before our military power had become strong, and especially in its dawn in the west, the tribes supposed all to be feeble and necessarily submissive who did not resist, and non-resistance, of course, produced mischief. They measured us by their only standard of savage morality—revenge; a law bloody indeed, but which the honest historian is forced to regard in considering the early years of nations, especially when the Indian and the unprotected white man come first in contact, and when perhaps the moral grade and the surrounding circumstances of both races are properly considered.

In order to judge justly, he who writes history must endeavor to make himself a man of the time he describes. He is unfair, if he decides on the events of the eighteenth century by the standards of the nineteenth. It would no doubt be considered infamous in Massachusetts, at the present day, if an Indian was killed, yet it is recorded, that in the early part of the last century, the general court of the province offered a bounty of £100 for every Indian's scalp. The cruel murders almost daily committed by the barbarians upon the defenseless frontier inhabitants, originated and were held to justify this enactment; and in one of the bloody onslaughts of the Massachusetts men against the savages, forty white warriors returned to Boston with ten scalps extended on hoops in Indian style, and demanded the reward of £1,000, which was promptly paid.

Nor were these expeditions against the red men unsanctified by prayer. Chaplains accompanied the doughty fighters. Early on the day of the conflict these pastors of the flock militant lifted up their voices, and declaring that they had "come *out* to meet the enemy, besought God that they might find him. They trusted Providence with their lives, and would rather die for their country than return if they could, without seeing the foe, and be called cowards for their pains!"

It might be supposed that these valiant clergymen contented themselves with beseeching the God of battles, and refrained from mingling in the fray. But this was not the case, for in the old ballad of the Fight at Pequawket, it is metrically narrated that:

"Our worthy Captain Love well
Among them there did die;
They, killed Lieutenant Robbins,

And wounded good young Frye,
Who was our English Chaplain;

He many Indians slew,
And some of them he scalped

While bullets round him flew!" *

* Drake's *Book of the Indians,* book III, pp. 128, 130, 133.

As his Britannic majesty's troops on the Ohio, at the epoch of which I have been speaking, had perhaps neither the power nor spirit to punish or reclaim the Indians and enforce the peace and the treaty, mischief became habitual among the tribes when they found that they escaped with impunity.* And, thus, in truth, the Indian hatchet was never buried. The summer after Bouquet's treaty, the savages killed a white man upon the Virginia frontiers; the next year, eight Virginians were butchered on the Cumberland, and their peltries brought to the Indian towns where they were sold to Pennsylvania traders. Sometime after, Martin, a Virginia trader, with two companions, was killed by the Shawanese on the Hockhocking; only, as it was alleged by Lord Dunmore, because they were Virginians; at the same time that the savages allowed a certain Ellis to pass simply because he was a Pennsylvanian. In 1771, twenty Virginians and their party of friendly Indians were robbed by savages of thirty-eight horses, as well as of weapons, clothes and trappings, which they delivered to Callender and Spears, and certain other Pennsylvania traders in their towns. In the same year, within the jurisdiction of Virginia, the Indians killed two remote settlers; and, in the following year Adam Stroud, another Virginian, with his wife and seven children, fell beneath their tomahawks and scalping knives on the waters of the Elk. In 1773, the savages were still engaged in their work of destruction. Richards fell on the Kanawha; and a few months after Russell, another Virginian, with five whites and two negroes, perished near the Cumberland Gap,** while their horses and property were borne off by the Indians to the towns where they fell a prey to the Pennsylvania traders. These and many other butcheries and robberies of a similar character, were committed in the savage raids and forays, anterior the year 1774, and long before Shawanese blood was wantonly shed in retaliation by the irritated people.*** A Dutch family was massacred on the Kanawha in June of 1773, and the family of Mr. Hog, and three white men, on the Great Kanawha, early in April, 1774.3 On the 25th of April, 1774, the Earl of Dunmore, at Williamsburg his seat of government in Virginia, issued his proclamation, which, as dates are of great importance in this narrative, we should regard as unveiling other causes of border difficulty, besides the Indian hostilities, which were then occurring.

* This was the rear of Boone's party in October, 1773. Some of Boone's sons were among the slain.

** Earl of Dunmore's Speech to the Delawares and Six Nation Chiefs, *Am. Archives,* 4th series, vol. I, p. 873.

*** *Am. Archives,* 4th series, vol. I, p. 1,015, and see also Lord Dunmore's answer, dated at Williamsburg, 29 May, 1774, to the speech of the Indians dated at Pittsburgh, May, 7, 1774, *Am. Arch., ut supra,* p. 482 ; but compare the alleged Indian statements contained in a letter dated 29 May, 1774, from Arthur St. Clair to Governor Penn, in the same volume, p. 286. See also Wither's *Chronicle of Border Warfare.*

It will be remembered, as I have already stated, that the territorial claim of Virginia covered at that time a large part of western Pennsylvania, and that a sharp controversy had arisen between the two provinces and their respective authorities, especially as to the domain commanding the navigable head waters on the line of frontier posts. There was great jealousy on both sides. The Virginia pioneer— planter, hunter and agriculturist — had met in conflict with the Pennsylvania trader. The Indians — as we have seen in the statement I gave of some of the murders during the ten years after Bouquet's peace — molested the Virginia forester, but appear to have spared the Pennsylvania trader. The allegations of Lord Dunmore in one of his speeches to the Indians, already referred to, exhibit the soreness of provincial feeling on this subject.* In this proclamation of the 25th of April, 1774, before there could possibly have been a communication of any retaliatory murders on the Ohio, committed by the whites upon the Indians, the British earl, then at Williamsburg, declares, that inasmuch as there is trouble within his jurisdiction at Pittsburgh, and the authorities in that place and its dependencies will endeavor to obstruct his majesty's government thereof by illegal means; and inasmuch as that "settlement is in danger of annoyance from Indians, also," he has thought proper, with the advice and consent of his majesty's counsel, to require and authorize the militia officers of that district to embody a sufficient number of men to repel *any assault whatever?* The events that caused the issuing of this proclamation must necessarily have occurred both among the white and the red men, a considerable time before, so as to have allowed the messenger to cross the mountains prior to the 25th of April.

* *American Archives, ut antea*, p. 482. *-Ibid*, 4th series, vol. I, p. 283. *Lord Dunmore's Proclamation.*

But even anterior to this, on the 24th of March, 1774, there was a letter published in the *Williamsburg Gazette,* addressed to the earl, and signed Virginius, warning him of an Indian war, and beseeching him to convoke the house of burgesses in order to raise men and means for the defense of the frontier.* The first volume of the fourth series of the *American Archives,* published; by congress, is full of narratives and official correspondence or minutes, disclosing the acrimonious provincial animosities as to western jurisdiction between Pennsylvania and Virginia at this time, and one writer declares that "more is to be dreaded from the rancorous feeling between the settlers from the two states than from the barbarians." The same volume contains numerous documents revealing the violent scenes that occurred in 1774, upon the arrival at Pittsburgh of John Connolly, who though a native of Lancaster County, in Pennsylvania, was regularly commissioned by Lord Dunmore, to represent his authority as a magistrate for West Augusta.**

* *American Archives*, 4th series, vol. I, p. 272 in the notes.

** See as to the causes of this war, in confirmation, Wither's *Chronicles of Border War/are*, chapter vi. He is decidedly of opinion that it was not caused by the murders at Captina Creek and opposite the mouth of Yellow Creek, which will be subsequently narrated. See *Almon's Remembrances*, vol. II, pp. 218,330. Smyth's *Travels in America*, Dublin, 1784. Smyth was one of Connolly's captured parties. Jacob's *Cresap*, p. 67. *American Archives*, vol. III. 1191-1192. Lord Dunmore was certainly good authority, at least for the fact that it was not "Cresap's War," as it has been called by some writers. The following MS. extract was sent to me by Mr. George Bancroft.

"Lord Dunmore to General Haldimand:
"Williamsburg, 24 *December*, 1774.

"Sir: I have received from Lord Dartmouth, an extract of a letter of which the inclosed is a copy.

"You have been very much imposed upon by the account given you which you thought fit to transmit to his Majesty's Minister. There is no other Colonel Cressop, than an old man of ninety years of age, who has not removed from his habitation for many years — for some from my own knowledge—and for the rest from incontestible authority. There is, indeed, one Michael Cressop (not a colonel but a trader), who, with others, *is said* to have killed those Indians (not on a scout but) returning from the back settlements *where he had been on his private business, and, where he found the Indians ravaging the country, and murdering every white man they could lay their hands on, and, therefore, very far from, being the cause of a war as you would suggest, or, even of hostilities. It was the consequence of repeated hostilities committed by the Indians on the people of our Frontiers; and both these Cressops are not Virginians, or even inhabited Virginia, but belonging to Maryland — with respect, however, to which, or, the cause of the war with the Indians, I conceive it not necessary for me to send you proofs."*

It is not a little singular, even if nothing more than a coincidence, that Lord Dunmore should have chosen the epoch of a menaced Indian war, and of a growing dispute with the mother country beyond the seas, to assert the rights of Virginia, not only by issuing his proclamation, but by dispatching to the scene of action a man like John Connolly, who was well known not only for his bold, restless and artful character, but for his sagacity, his knowledge of the world and of Indian affairs, and his exceedingly lax morality.*

* Burk's *Hist. Virginia,* vol. Ill, p. 374, and vol. IV, p. 74. At the latter reference the reader will find a further development of Connolly's subsequent conduct and hostility to American interests, as disclosed in the plot formed by Lord Dunmore to bring the Indian tribes of the west into the revolutionary conflict. Connolly, on his way to Detroit, was arrested near Fredericktown in Maryland, by the committee of safety; was examined and committed to close custody on the 23d November, 1775. He had been commissioned by the earl, as a lieutenant colonel commandant.— *Burke,* vol. IV, appendix iv. The joint plans of these loyal Britons show the great probability that, in truth, there was a scheme in embryo to crush the American revolution at its birth, by a union between the Indians, negroes and loyalists, and by the excitement of an Indian war on the frontier, which would compel the settlers to think of self-protection against savages, instead of demanding from England the security of right and liberty, *c.t* the muzzle of the rifle. By a letter from Lord Dartmouth to Lord Dunmore, dated" at Whitehall on the 2d of August, 1775, it appears that, *in the previous May,* Dunmore had communicated to the home government his vile plan of raising the Indians and negroes to join the miscalled loyalists in an onslaught against the Americans. The following letter, a copy of which has been very kindly sent to me by Mr. George Bancroft, is probably the one of the "previous May" alluded to:

(Extract).
"Williamsburg, *1st May,* 1775.

"If the Servants of the Crown should be of opinion that the authority of the government ought to be enforced here, I am persuaded, that if his Majesty should think proper to add to the small body of troops to be sent here, a quantity of arms and ammunition and other requisites for the Service, I could raise such a force from among Indians, as our history would soon reduce the refractory people of this Colony to obedience."— *State Paper office, London: Virginia,* vol. CXC V.

See also *Sabine's Loyalists,* article, John Connolly.

The original papers relative to the arrest of Connolly and his incendiary companions in Maryland in 1775 are recorded in the MS. *Journal of the Committee of Observation of the Middle District of Frederick County,* under date of the 21 Nov., 1775, in the possession of the Maryland Historical Society. This record gives, 1st, The letter from John Connolly to John Gibson, dated at Portsmouth, Aug. 9, 1775: 2d, A letter from Lord Dunmore to the Indian Capt. White Eyes. It contains a *loving* message to *"his brother"* The Cornstalk (the same who had fought at Pt. Pleasant): 3d, Proposals to General Gage for raising an army to the westward for the purpose of effectually obstructing a communication between the southern and northern governments. One of the chief proposals was to raise the Indians.

See Letters from, Arthur St. Clair to Gov. Penn, Ligonier, 29 May, 1774, *Am. Arch.,* 4th series, vol. I, p. 287.

This is not a proper occasion to discuss a border controversy between the two great provinces which has never yet been fully chronicled, and, at best, could only be an episode in our history. Yet I have thought it right to show that it occurred, singularly enough, just at the epoch of the wars of 1774 and of the revolution, and was probably considered as a means of exciting enmity and disaffection betwixt Virginians and Pennsylvanians, of loosening the links between two vast territorial empires, and thus of weakening the sympathetic bond which should have bound all Americans at that critical moment. The fatal quarrel with Great Britain had already begun, and all the chief provinces from Massachusetts southward, were rallying in the general national cause with a firmness that betokened danger to the dominion of the parent state unless our liberties were left untouched.

But there is a third motive for this war which we admit is not altogether proved against the British earl, although there are facts that strongly fortify the belief entertained on the subject by early American writers and soldiers who served in the campaign. Among all the authors and journalists of the war there is evidently a strong impression, amounting almost to positive conviction, that Connolly, as the tool of Dunmore, secretly fomented the war with ulterior views, as a counter irritation against the menaced resistance to England. Those who lived nearest the scene of action, and especially the Virginians who had the best means of judging Dunmore's motives, believed from circumstances that transpired during the conflict, that the Indians were urged to a war by the instigation of emissaries from Great Britain and by the Canadian traders. It was generally credited that Dunmore had received from England advices concerning the approaching contest, and that all his measures with the Indians had for their ultimate object an alliance *of foreign troops and loyalists* with the ferocious warriors against the Americans. Nothing, indeed, was more natural than for British politicians at home to suppose that the excitement of an Indian war, and a contemporary dissension between the people of two large provinces in America, would be the means of preventing a colonial coalition in opposition to parliamentary taxation.* But, fortunately for our liberties, the alarm of an Indian war neither palsied nor benumbed the masses. And although Pennsylvania did not contribute largely to its suppression, it was not until the military ardor and indignation of the people throughout Virginia blazed up in the colony and reacted on Dunmore, that he affected, at least, to feel a hectic glow of virtuous indignation, and placed himself at the head of the troops that gathered from every glen and mountain to repel the savage. **

* Burk's *Hist. Virg.,* vol. Ill, p. 380 ; Wither's *Chronicles,* p. 107; Dr. Doddridge's account of Dunmore's war in *Kercheval* (edition of 1833), p. 157; Rev. Mr. Jacob's *Life of Cresap,* pp. 47, 52, 53, 67; Col. Stuart's *Memoir of the Indian Wars,* printed by the Virginia Historical Society, pp. 41, 43, 49, 56; Howison's *History Virginia,* vol. II, p. 72; Hildreth's *History U. States,* vol. Ill, p. 49 ; Monette's *History Valley of the Mississippi,* vol. I, p. 385; *Virginia Historical Register,* vol. I, p 32, in Col. Andrew Lewis's letter; *Annals of the West; Ohio Historical Collections,* by Howe, p. 408; *Almon's Remembrancer,* vol. II, pp. 218, 330;

Smyth's *Travels in America,* Dublin, 1784. As to Dunmore's supposed treachery see *Am. Arch.,* 4th series, vol. Ill, pp. 1191, 1192, for some strong suspicions on this point from facts that became known after the treaty of Camp Charlotte and the close of the campaign.

** *Burk,* vol. Ill, p. 381. The *Pennsylvania authorities* took precautions soon after the outbreak of troubles to signify to the Indians, by messengers, that the alleged outrages were *not committed by Pennsylvanians,* and that the government of *Pennsylvania disavowed and condemned them, and therefore were not proper objects of revenge.* This timely notice is probably the reason why the Indian war was not carried on against the frontier settlements of Pennsylvania, but was chiefly directed against those of Virginia, where all kinds of savage barbarities were inflicted. See Gordon's *History of Pennsylvania,* p. 475; Monette's *Valley of the Mississippi,* vol. I, p. 371. See also Drake's *Book of the Indians,* book v, p. 45, for some sound reasoning on Dunmore's conduct.

It will be perceived, therefore, that there were three probable causes or motives for the war which broke out in 1774, the leading events of which I will narrate very briefly.

I. The hostility of the Indians had been constantly manifested in the most murderous and predatory manner ever since Bouquet's peace in 1764; and, at the same time, the gradual enlargement of the white settlements had brought, in perilous neighborhood, two races who were naturally hostile, while neither the savages of the one, nor the hardy woodsmen of the other, were prepared, by continuous forbearance, to avoid conflict or to unite in a common tenure of the soil.

II. The Pennsylvania disputes with Virginia as to territorial limits and jurisdiction were unwisely fomented by the forcible acts of Dunmore and Connolly, and thus the comity and good-will between two of the most important colonies were fearfully endangered.

III. It was probably Lord Dunmore's desire to incite a war which would arouse and band the savages of the west, so that, in the anticipated struggle with the United Colonies, the British *home interest* might ultimately avail itself of these children of the forest as ferocious and formidable allies in the onslaught on the Americans. But, at all events, nothing, so well as the Indian border war, would produce a counteraction in the land at this moment of peril, and absorb the colonist in the exclusive duty of self-protection against a foe that was more to be feared than parliamentary taxation.

From this brief view of the political field of the colonies in 1774, let us return to the scene of impending hostilities.

We left Michael Cresap, the western frontier trader, a man of broken fortunes, emigrating from his Maryland homestead among the mountains of Cumberland, to the broad lands and pleasant valleys of the Ohio. His purpose unquestionably was not warlike; for, in the disastrous condition of his affairs, and with a large family to maintain, peace was absolutely necessary for success in his new field of enterprise. Accordingly, early in 1774, we find him on the Ohio River, in the neighborhood of Pittsburgh and Wheeling, with laborers brought under contract of hire from Maryland, engaged in opening and locating farms. He was there neither as a speculator nor a land-jobber, as many of the emigrants of those days were unjustly stigmatized. His purpose was peaceful settlement, and he is no more to be blamed for his manly progress into the wilderness in quest of land, than were Washington and many other distinguished Americans of those days who possessed themselves of property in the prolific valleys of the west.*

* Historians have been in the habit of stigmatizing all concerned in the outbreak of the war as speculators and land-jobbers who were anxious to drive off the Indians. I shall insert below an advertisement from the *Maryland Gazette* of May 26, 1774, which shows the opinion, at least of Washington, at that time, and is surely calculated to prove the honesty of purpose with which far-seeing men took advantage of their opportunities to obtain titles and open farms in the region beyond the Alleghenies:

"Fairfax County, Va., *May* 10, 1774.

"In the month of March last the subscribers sent out a number of carpenters and laborers, to build houses and clear and enclose lands on the Ohio, intending to divide the several tracts which he there holds, into convenient sized tenements and to give leases therefor for lives, or a term of years, renewable forever, under certain conditions which may be known either of him. or Mr. Valentine Crawford, who is now on the land.

"The situation and quality of these lands having been thoroughly described in a former advertisement, it is unnecessary to enlarge on them here; suffice it generally to observe, that there are no better in that country, and that the whole of them lay upon the banks either of the Ohio or Great Kanawha, and are capable of receiving the highest improvement.

"George Washington."

Cresap was engaged in these honest and laudable pursuits when he suddenly received a summons which terminated his agricultural projects in the west.

After this region had been explored in 1773, a resolution was formed by a band of hardy pioneers—among whom was George Rogers Clark, who, afterwards, as a general officer, became so celebrated in the annals of Kentucky— to make a settlement during the following spring; and the mouth of the little Kanawha was appointed as the place of general rendezvous, whence the united party should descend the river. Early in 1774 the Indians had done some of their habitual mischief. Reports of further and perhaps meditated dangers were rife along the river, as coming from the Indian towns. Many of the promised settlers, alarmed by the news, remained at their homes, so that, at the appointed time, not more than eighty or ninety men assembled at the rendezvous.

In a few days the anticipated troubles with the savages commenced. A small party of hunters, encamped about ten miles below Clark's emigrants, was fired on by the Indians; but the red men were repulsed and the hunters returned to camp. This hostile demonstration, coupled with the rumors already spoken of, satisfied the Americans that the savages were bent on war. Accordingly, the whole band was regularly enrolled for protection; yet it was resolved to adhere to the original project of settling in Kentucky, inasmuch as the camp was amply furnished with everything needful for such an enterprise.

An Indian town, called the Horse-head Bottom, on the Scioto, near its mouth, lay in the pioneers' way, and they forthwith resolved to cross the country and surprise it. But when the question arose as to who should command so perilous an adventure, it was found that in the whole band, no one possessed sufficient experience in Indian warfare to be entrusted confidently with the fortunes of his companions. It was known, however, that Michael Cresap dwelt on the river about fifteen miles above the camp, engaged with certain laborers in settling a plantation, and that he had resolved to follow this band of pioneers to Kentucky as soon as he had established his people. His experience of frontier life was notorious. The eager settlers, with one voice, resolved to demand his services in the hour of danger, and a messenger was forthwith dispatched to seek him. In half an hour he returned with Michael, who, hearing of the unwise resolution to attack the Indian town had already set out to visit the pioneer camp. The emigrants at once thought their army, as they called it, complete, and the destruction of the savages certain.

But a council was called, and to the surprise of all, the intended commander-in-chief promptly dissuaded his companions from the meditated enterprise. He said that, in truth, appearances were very suspicious, yet there was no certainty of war; that if the pioneers attacked the savages he had no doubt of success, but that a war would be the unquestionable result, the blame of which would fall upon the assailants. If they determined to proceed, however, he promised to send to his camp for his people, and to share the fortunes of the adventurers.

This mild but resolute counsel struck the whole band forcibly, and it was immediately resolved, according to Cresap's advice, to return to Wheeling as a convenient post where further tidings might readily be obtained. A few weeks, he thought, would determine the impending issue; and, as it was still early in the spring, if the Indians were found to be indisposed for war, the emigrants would have ample time to descend the river to their proposed settlement in Kentucky.

In two hours the pioneers had struck their tents and were on their way to Wheeling. As they ascended the river they met Killbuck, an Indian chief, accompanied by a small party; and had a long but unsatisfactory interview with him as to the disposition of the tribes. It was observed that Cresap did not attend this conference, but remained on the opposite side of the river, declaring that he was afraid to trust himself with the Indians, especially as Killbuck had frequently attempted to waylay and murder his father in Maryland, and that if they met, his fortitude might forsake him and he might put the savage to death.1 These anecdotes denote the caution and self-restraint, the prudence and vigilance with which Michael Cresap behaved and counseled during the whole of these opening scenes, and exhibit him in the true light of an emigrant who was anxious to maintain inviolate the peace of a region in which his fortunes had been cast.

*Killbuck — see Jacob's *Life of Cresap,* p. 31, for a ludicrous *accident* that happened to this Indian whilst engaged in the assault upon Cresap and his friends at the Old Town affair heretofore narrated. It was perhaps the first time that a savage was so singularly *wounded* by a woman!

On the party's arrival at Wheeling, around which there were many white settlements, all the inhabitants appeared to be alarmed. They flocked to the camp from every direction, and refused to leave the protecting wings of the pioneers. Offers were made to cover their neighborhood with scouts, until further reliable information was received; but no counsel or promise of protection would avail. Every day brought fresh accessions of strength to the party. Farmers, hunters,, woodsmen, flocked to the band of Kentucky pioneers, until its numbers became formidable.

The arrival of these men at Wheeling was soon known at Pittsburgh, and the whole of that region, as I have stated, was, under the asserted jurisdiction of Virginia, controlled by Connolly, under Dunmore's commission for West Augusta. When Connolly heard of the pioneers' approach to Wheeling he sent a message to the party, informing it that war was to be apprehended, and requesting that it would remain in position a short time inasmuch as messages had been sent to the Indians and a few days would solve the doubt. Before a complying answer could reach Pittsburgh, however, a second express arrived from Connolly, addressed to Captain Cresap, as the most influential man in the band, apprizing him that the messengers had returned from the Indians, that war was inevitable, that the savages would strike as soon as the season permitted, and begging him to use his influence with the party to cover the country with scouts until the inhabitants could fortify themselves.* This message reached Cresap about the 21st of April,** and its reception was the signal for open hostilities against the Indians. Such was the natural result on so exposed a frontier, where the white man or the savage who obtained the first shot was the victor, and where the Indian assassination or private war—to give it the most civilized name—was the only rule recognized by the red men when they were aroused against encroaching Americans.

*Jacob's *Life of Cresap,* p. 54; *Am. Archives,* 4th series, vol. I, p. 468 ; Gen. Rogers Clarke's letter in the appendix No. 1 to this discourse. Dr. Wheeler's testimony in *Jacob,* p. 110.

**The letter in the *American Archives* referred to above at p. 468, indicates the date of this letter or message from Connolly to have been on the 21st *of April,* 1774. Devereux Smith writes to Dr. Smith from Pittsburgh under date of 10th of June, 1774, as follows: "On the 21st of April Connolly wrote a letter to the inhabitants of Wheeling, telling them that he had been informed by good authority that the Shawanese were ill-disposed towards white men, and he therefore required and commanded them to hold themselves in readiness to repel any insults that might be offered them." See also same volume of *Am. Arch.,* p. 287, where Connolly's "circular letter to the inhabitants on the *Ohio"* is spoken of. *Jacob* says *he once possessed it:* pp 53, 54, 110, 113.

The time of the reception of Connolly's letter was thus the date of hostilities against the Indians. A new post was immediately planted, a council called, and the letter read not only to the military party but to all the neighboring Indian traders who were summoned on so important an occasion. The result was a solemn and formal declaration of war on the 26th of April, and that very night two scalps were brought into the camp.*

* McKee's MS. Journal, *London Documents*, Albany, N. Y. *Am. Arch.*, 4th series, vol. I, p. 345.

Some days prior to this, Mr. William Butler, who seems not to have heeded the earlier warnings, had sent off a canoe loaded with goods for the Shawanese towns, and on the 16th of April, it was attacked, forty miles below Pittsburgh by three Cherokees, who waylaid it on the river. They killed one white man, wounded another and a third made his escape, while the savages plundered the canoe of the most valuable part of the cargo.

The day after the declaration of war by Cresap and his men, under the warning authority of Connolly's message, some canoes of Indians were descried on the river keeping under the cover of an island to screen themselves from the party's sight. The skiffs were immediately chased fifteen miles down the river, and driven on shore. A battle ensued, in which an Indian was taken prisoner; a few were wounded on both sides, and perhaps one slain. On examining the canoes they were found to contain a considerable quantity of ammunition and other warlike stores.*

* Sec Alex. McKee's MS. Journal, *London Documents,* Albany, and article in *Am. Jour, of Science and Art,* for October, 1846, p. 10; and compare with the letter in appendix No. 1 to this discourse.

In the deliberations of the camp on the night after the party's return, it was determined that a band should march on the following morning about thirty miles up the river in order to attack the settlement of Logan; but the band had not advanced more than five miles, when, halting for refreshment, Cresap asserted the gross impropriety of executing so dastardly an enterprise against a party composed of men, women and children who were known to cherish no hostile intentions but to be solely engaged in hunting. These facts were familiar to the pioneers, many of whom had visited the Indian camp during the preceding March, as they descended the Ohio to their original rendezvous.

Cresap's counsel immediately prevailed, and every man present seemed disgusted with a project which, a short time before, had been so heedlessly and shamefully cherished. The party returned to camp in the evening, and speedily took the road to Red-Stone Old Fort.*

* See General Clark's letter; appendix No. 1. This important letter *now published for the first time from the original in the Jefferson Papers,* in the archives of the state department at Washington, is the most authentic account of the transactions preceding this Indian war, as well as of the treaty at its conclusion. The character of its author is too well known to require elucidation.

Thus, Cresap and his men were gone from the scene; but unfortunately, his prudent and friendly advice as to the settlement of Logan was not heeded by other adventurers on the river. On the last day of April, 1774, it was cruelly destroyed by others.*

* See General Clark's letter, appendix No. 1.— Benjamin Tomlinson, in his testimony in Jacob's *Life of Cresap*, p. 107, fixes the time on the "third or fourth of May; but John Sappington's statement in the 4th appendix to Jefferson's *Notes on Va.*, p. 52, dates it on the 24th of May. I am satisfied the massacre occurred on the 30th of April, 1774, and that Sappington's date of the 24th May, *given from memory, after a lapse of twenty-six years,* is inaccurate. An examination of Washington's MSS. in the archives of the state department at Washington has disclosed a letter from Valentine Crawford to Colonel G. Washington, from Jacob's Creek on the Monongahela and dated "May 7th, 1774." The following is an extract from it. After describing some of the Indian and pioneer fights posterior to the Yellow Creek massacre, he adds: "And on *Saturday last,* about twelve o'clock, there was one Greathouse and about twenty men fell on a party of Indians at the mouth of Yellow Creek, and killed ten of them, and brought away one child a prisoner, which is now at my brother William Crawford's." By reference to the Almanac for 1774, it will be seen that the Saturday before the 7th of May of that year—the date of Valentine Crawford's letter — was *the 30th of April.* Valentine Crawford was Washington's land-agent, in the west.

The Indian camp was about thirty miles above Wheeling, close to the mouth of Yellow Creek, while on the opposite side of the Ohio, near the river bank, was the cabin of a certain Baker, who sold rum to the Indians, and of course received frequent visits from them.

This man had been particularly desired by Cresap to remove his liquors, and seems to have prepared to take them away at the time of the murder.

Towards the close of April, 1774, a certain Michael Myers —who still lived on the Ohio a few miles above Steubenville, in February, 1850—resided on Pigeon creek, which, according to the maps, lies about forty miles from Yellow Creek. In consequence of Indian alarms, Myers was called forth from this settlement to go with his neighbors to guard the frontier at Baker's Bottom. While there, two land hunters induced him to accompany them across the stream and along the banks of this Yellow Creek in order to examine the country. Proceeding by the western shore of the creek for some miles, the travelers bivouacked for the night, and hobbled the only horse they had with them so as to prevent his straying far from the camp. The animal, nevertheless, rambled off about three hundred yards out of sight, over a rising ground; and, soon after, the woodsmen hearing the beast's bell rattle violently, seized their guns and started to discover the cause. On reaching the top of the ridge, Myers beheld near forty yards below, an Indian in the act of loosening the horse which seemed restive and anxious to break from the savage whose gun lay on the ground beside him. Myers, crouching behind the hillock, instantly leveled his rifle and shot the Indian. It was now a little after sunset, and soon, another Indian, attracted by the crack of the weapon, approached rapidly armed with his rifle, but halted abruptly in astonishment as soon as he beheld his prostrate fellow. In the meanwhile Myers had reloaded his rifle, and before the savage could recover from his surprise, he too, fell before the forester's fatal aim. In the distance the camp of the clan, spread with deer and bearskins, was visible, and as prompt succor was at hand, the Americans did not pause to see whether the Indian's wounds were deadly, but flying from the spot, re-crossed the Ohio for safety, and hastened to the neighborhood of Baker's cabin.* The evening or night, before the tragedy which I am now about to narrate was committed at this cabin, a squaw came over to Baker's and aroused the attention of the inmates by her tears and distress. For a long time she refused to disclose the cause of her sorrow, but at last, when left alone with Baker's wife, confessed that the Indians had resolved to kill the white woman and her family the next day; but, as she loved her and did not wish to see her slain, she had crossed the river to divulge the plot so as to enable her friend to escape. The savages had most probably been roused to revenge by the unfortunate encounter of Myers with their clansmen.

* MS. narrative sent to me by Mr. L. C. Draper, who visited Myers in 1850, and received the account from his lips. Mr. D. thinks that the narrator *may* have confounded in his memory the events of another period; but as Myers *positively asserts that this affair led the hostile parties of Indians to go over next day to Baker's; as it gives the plausible pretext for the story of the squaw who visited Mrs. Baker; and, as it is the same that Myers has constantly told his neighbors,* I am inclined to rely in its accuracy. Mr. Myers has always sustained a good character; in early times was a captain, and served as a justice of the peace for many years. Myers admits that he took part in firing on the Indians who crossed in canoes on the day of the massacre.

In consequence of this information, and in dread of the meditated assassination, Baker summoned a number of his neighbors, who all reached his house before morning, when it was resolved that the strangers should conceal themselves in a back apartment, whence the assailing Indians might be watched. It was also determined that if they demeaned themselves peaceably, they should not be molested; but if hostility was manifested, they should show themselves and act accordingly.*

*Some writers declare that Greathouse visited the Indian camp the night before the massacre and "decoyed" the savages over to drink on the next day. McKee's *JUS. Journal, ut antea. Moravian Journal, Am. Arch.,* vol. I, p. 285.

Early in the morning a party of eight Indians, composed of three squaws, a child, and four unarmed men, one of whom was Logan's brother, crossed the river to Baker's cabin, where all but Logan's brother obtained liquor and became excessively drunk. No whites, except Baker and two of his companions appeared in the cabin. After some time Logan's relative took down a coat and hat belonging to Baker's brother-in-law, and putting them on, set his arms akimbo, strutted about the apartment, and at length coming up abruptly to one of the men, addressed him with the most offensive epithets and attempted to strike him.* The white man — Sappington** — who was thus assailed by language and gesture, for some time kept out of his way; but becoming irritated, seized his gun and shot the Indian as he was rushing to the door still clad in the coat and hat. The men, who during the whole of this scene had remained hidden, now poured forth, and, without parley slaughtered the whole Indian party except the child. Before this tragic event occurred, two canoes, one with two and the other with five Indians, all naked, painted, and completely armed for war, were descried stealing from the opposite shore where Logan's camp was situated. This was considered as confirmation of what the squaw had said the night before, and was afterwards alleged in justification of the murder of the unarmed party which had first arrived.

* See Withers's *Border Warfare*, p. 113, for Col. Swearingen's testimony as to the provoking conduct of Logan's brother at Yellow Creek, and as to the origin of this affair.

** See McKee's certificate, in *Jefferson*, at the end of Sappington's narrative.

No sooner were the unresisting drunkards dead, than the infuriated whites rushed to the river bank and ranging themselves along the concealing fringe of underwood, prepared to receive the canoes. The first that arrived was the one containing two warriors, who were fired upon and killed. The other canoe immediately turned and fled; but after this, two others containing eighteen warriors, painted and prepared for conflict as the first had been, started to assail the Americans. Advancing more cautiously than the former party, they endeavored to land below Baker's cabin, but being met by the rapid movements of the rangers before they could effect their purpose, they were put to flight with the loss of one man, although they returned the fire of the pioneers.

In this desperate and bloody massacre, which was hastily perpetrated it seems in anticipation of an Indian attack, an anticipation which was probably confirmed by the opportune appearance of the armed and painted warriors, there were several men by the name of Greathouse deeply and fearfully concerned. There are persons who charge the whole of the horrid action upon these individuals, yet its details are too disgusting to be dwelt on more than is needed in characterizing a single event of those cruel times.* John Sappington, whose statement in the ivth appendix to Jefferson's *Notes on Virginia* is the clearest, most circumstantial and consistent that I found in the volume, declares that he does not *believe* Logan had any relations killed, except a brother; that none of the squaws who were slain was his wife; that two of them were old women, while the third, whose infant was spared, was the wife of General Gibson, who, at that period was an Indian trader, and subsequently took care of the child as if it had been his own.

* See and compare: John Sappington's statement in Jefferson's *Notes on Virginia,* appendix No. iv, p. 51; James Chambers's deposition, *id.— id.,* p. 39; Robinson's at p. 42; Gen. Clark's letter, appendix No. 1 to this discourse. Sappington states that he was " intimately acquainted with all the circumstances respecting the destruction of Logan's family," though he does not admit, in his carefully drawn statement, that he was *present* at the scene of murder. McKee in his certificate appended to Sappington's testimony in Jefferson's *Notes,* says that Sappington admitted he was the man who killed Logan's brother. See also the statement written by Mr. Jolly, published in the *American Journal of Science and Arts,* vol. XXXI, p. 10, and republished in Howe's *Ohio Hist. Coll.,* 266. See Drake's *Book of the Indians.*

It is important to recollect that all these statements and depositions positively prove that Captain Michael Cresap was neither present at nor countenanced the alleged murder of Logan's kin at the Yellow Creek massacre. The fact that *Sappington's* statement was published *by Mr. Jefferson himself* indicates the confidence he placed in it, especially as he inserts it as a sort of supplement to the other testimony on the subject which had been printed *before* its reception. Logan's mother, brother, and sister (Gibson's Indian wife or squaw, in all likelihood), were, probably, all of the relatives of Logan killed there.

In Jacob's *Life of Cresap,* page 108, Jacob Tomlinson, (whose character for veracity is strongly authenticated in the *Olden Time,* vol. II, p. 475, &c), states that the attacking party, at Baker's Bottom, had no commander.

"I believe," he continues, *"Logan's brother was killed by a man named Sappington;* who killed the others I know not, *although I was present;* but this I know well, that neither Captain Michael Cresap, nor any other person of that name was there, nor do I believe, within many miles of the place." The statement in the *Olden Time* is to the same effect in exculpation of Cresap, but in that work it is not Tomlinson's direct testimony, signed by him, as that was which Jacob reports, but the relation from memory of his convictions on the subject.

The war soon raged. This act seems to have roused the Indians to immediate hostility. A letter from Arthur St. Clair to Governor Penn, dated at Ligonier, on the 22d of June, states that Logan is returned with one prisoner and thirteen scalps.* The blood of his kindred cried for vengeance and he had already trod the warpath.

* *Am. Archives,* 4th series, vol. I, p. 475.

On the 12th of July, as William Robinson, Thomas Hellen and Coleman Brown, were gathering flax in a field, on the west fork of the Monongahela, they were surprised by a party of eight Indians, led by Logan. The savages stole upon them and fired before they were perceived. Brown fell, pierced by several balls, but Hellen and Robinson sought safety in flight. Hellen was too old to avoid capture; yet Robinson, with the agility of youth, and urged by his love of life and liberty, would have escaped but for an untoward accident. Believing that he was outstripping his pursuers in the race, he hastily turned to ascertain the fact, but while glancing over his shoulder, he ran with such violence against a tree as to be thrown stunned and powerless on the ground. The savages at once secured him with cords, and when revived, he was taken back to the spot where the lifeless and bleeding body of Brown was laid, and where Hellen was already secured. Taking with them a horse belonging to the latter, the Indians immediately departed for their towns with the prisoners.

As they approached the Indian camp Logan gave the scalp halloo, and, immediately, several warriors came forth to meet them. The unfortunate captives were now compelled to run the gauntlet for their lives. Logan had manifested a kindly feeling to Robinson from the moment of his seizure, and instructed him as to the way by which he might reach the Council House of the clan without danger. But the decrepit Hellen, ignorant of the place of refuge, was sadly beaten before he arrived; and, when at length he had come almost within the asylum, he was prostrated with a war club before he could enter. "After he had fallen, the savages continued to beat him with such unmerciful severity that he would assuredly have died under their barbarous usage, had not Robinson, at some peril to his own safety for the interference, stretched forth his hand and dragged him within the sanctuary. When he recovered from the violent beating he was relieved from the apprehension of further suffering by adoption into an Indian family."

A council was next convoked to decide the fate of Robinson. Logan assured him that he should not be sacrificed; but the council appeared resolved on his death, and accordingly he was tied to the stake. His captor at once appealed to the warriors with great vehemence; insisted that Robinson should be spared; and poured forth a torrent of vehement eloquence, which, nevertheless, did not avail to avert his stern and dreadful sentence. At length, enraged at the pertinacity with which the life of Robinson, his own captive, was refused to him, and heedless of consequences, Logan drew the tomahawk from his belt, and cleaving the cords which bound the victim to the stake, hurried him to the wigwam of an ancient squaw, by whom he was at once adopted as a member of her family. He was to fill the place of a warrior who had been slain in the Yellow Creek massacre.*

*Withers's *Border Warfare*, 118, *et seq.*; Robinson's narrative in Jefferson's *Appendix*, iv, p. 41; Howe's *Ohio Hist. Coll.*, p. 267.

About three days after this occurrence, Logan suddenly brought to Robinson a piece of paper, and making a black fluid with water and gun powder, commanded him to write a note which we shall see was soon used in one of the brutal raids of the detached parties that scoured the country and laid waste every scattered and isolated settlement within a day's march of the Ohio. Men, women, children— and even cattle — were all indiscriminately scalped and butchered. The females were stripped and outraged. The men were slain, and knives, tomahawks or axes left in the breasts they had cleft asunder. The brains of infants were beaten out, and the carcasses left for the beasts of prey of the forest.*

* *Md. Gazette*, 30th June, 1774; Hite's account of the murder of Spier's family on the 3d or 4th of June. See also same paper of 30th Nov. for letter from Col. Preston at Fincastle, 28th Sept., describing Indian murders and outrages.

When Judge Innes happened to be at the residence of Colonel Preston's family, in the fall of 1774, an express was sent to the colonel as lieutenant of the County, requesting a guard of militia to be sent out for the protection of the residents on the lower portions of the north fork of the Holston. Every member of the family of a settler named John Roberts,* had been cruelly cut off by the savages, and the perpetrator of the assassination was traced by "the card" which he left as a bloody memorial of his visit! A war club was deposited in the house of the murdered forester, and, attached to it, was the following note—the identical one which Logan had forced Robinson to write with his gunpowder ink:

"Captain Cresap,

"What did you kill my people on Yellow Creek for? The white people killed my kin at Conestoga, a great while ago, and I thought nothing of that. But you killed my kin again on Yellow Creek, and took my cousin prisoner. Then I thought I must kill too; and I have been three times to war since; but the Indians are not angry, only myself.

"Captain John Logan.

"July 21st, 1774."

* Among the MS. papers of Col. Wm. Preston in the possession of Mr. L. C. Draper, there is an original letter from Major Arthur Campbell, dated the 12th of October, in which he enclosed a copy in Col. Preston's handwriting, of Logan's missive. This is doubtless the one to which Innes alludes in Jefferson's *Appendix.* The correct name was Roberts. Captain Anthony Bledsoe in a letter to Col. Preston, dated at Camp Union (now Lewisburg, Va.), October 15th,1774, says: "I understand by Mr. Jones that he saw letter at your house that was left at Roberts's subscribed by one Logan, directed to Cresap. There are two young men now in my company who say they know one Logan, *a mixtbreed,* in the Shawano nation; one of whom I can depend on, the other is a stranger; they both agree in statement as to Logan's being a notorious villain." MS. Letter among Col. Preston's papers.

The late Hon. Thomas H. Benton wrote to me in April, 1855: "Among the things cherished which I lost in the burning of my house was your vindication of Cresap from the charge of murdering Logan's family, and the object of this note is to ask if you could send me another copy." In acknowledging the receipt of one, Mr. Benton said: " I have always thought *the speech* was a little helped in its transition from Logan to us, but *the letter* tied on a war club, left in the house of the destroyed family of Roberts, is real Indian, and would verify itself without witnesses, but is an old acquaintance of mine. I married the granddaughter of Colonel Preston, to whom, as colonel of the County, the club and note were brought, and have often heard my mother-in-law—Mrs. McDowell—and others of the family, relate all the circumstances of its delivery to their father."

This is a document savagely circumstantial and circumstantially savage; cool, deliberate, and bloody, even to the date—and left as this Indian's apology—not as his challenge—in the desolated dwelling and amid the reeking bodies he had butchered. It is the first deliberate charge made by Logan of the supposed murder of his relatives by Cresap at Yellow Creek, and I must promptly rebuke it by recalling to the reader's mind all the facts of that occurrence, against which Cresap had protested to Clark's party, and from the scene of which he had drawn off his men and departed.

While these events were transpiring, Michael Cresap had not only left the Ohio River, but had returned to his family in Maryland. Yet, soon finding his sympathies were excited for the forlorn inhabitants of the wilderness which he had abandoned, and hearing constant reports of Indian cruelties, he speedily raised a company of volunteers and marched back to their assistance. Having reached Catfish's Camp, on the spot where Washington, in Pennsylvania, now stands, his advance was stopped by a peremptory and insulting letter from Connolly, in which he was ordered to dismiss his men. It was no doubt written by its base author in order to commence the systematic plan of charging the Indian difficulties of 1774 on Michael Cresap.

Offensive as was such a command to a person of Cresap's character, he nevertheless obeyed, returned to his home and dismissed his men, with the determination to take no part in the Indian war, but to let the commandant at Pittsburgh fight it out as he best could. It seems, however, that the Earl of Dunmore and his lieutenant at Pittsburgh did not agree as to the value of Michael's services, for, when Cresap reached his Maryland home he found Lord Dunmore at his house, where he tarried some days in friendly intercourse or consultation with the young pioneer; arid, notwithstanding his residence in Maryland, the British governor of Virginia saw fit to send him forthwith a commission as captain in the militia of Hampshire County. This appointment, dated on the 10th of June, reached Cresap opportunely, and, carrying with it, as an unsolicited favor, a tacit expression of the earl's approbation of his conduct, he resolved to accept it, especially as he was constantly appealed to by letters from his old companions beyond the mountains to hasten to their succor.

As soon as he raised his standard crowds flocked to it, and, indeed, so great was his popularity as a leader that his own command overflowed with men and enabled him to fill up completely the company of his nephew, and partly also the company of Hancock Lee. His forces were then united under the command of Major Angus McDonald, who had been, meanwhile, organizing the western people on the Youghiogheny and Monongahela for their own defense.

A campaign was also planned for the invasion of the Indian country west of the Ohio. "Orders were immediately sent to Colonel Andrew Lewis, of Botetourt County, to raise with all dispatch four regiments of militia and volunteers from the southwestern counties, to rendezvous at Camp Union in Greenbrier County. This was to be the southern division of the invading army, of which Lewis, a veteran of the French war, was made commander. He was ordered to march down the Great Kanawha to the bank of the Ohio, and there to join the earl in person. In the meantime Lord Dunmore was actively engaged in raising troops in the northern counties west of the Blue Ridge, to advance from Fort Cumberland by way of Redstone Old Fort, to the Ohio at Pittsburgh, whence he was to descend in boats to the Kanawha. Such was the original plan of the campaign."*

*Monette, vol. I, p. 374

McDonald, agreeably to Dunmore's orders, after a dreary march through the wilderness, had rendezvoused his four hundred men at Wheeling creek in June, and, from this place, it was resolved to invade the Indian Territory on the head waters of the Muskingum and to destroy the Wapatomica towns. The results of this expedition were not of remarkable value in the campaign, though the Indian towns were destroyed by the invaders after the savages fled. McDonald and his men were harassed by the foe, and being short of provisions, returned with dispatch to Wheeling.*

* Jacob's *Life of Cresap*, p. 375. As to McDonald's expedition, see *Am. Archives*, vol. I, p. 722, &c; *Doddridge, Withers, Kercheval, Jacob;* and Thomas's Reminiscences in Howe's *Ohio*, p. 382.

All the agricultural operations of the settlers on the river were of course broken up, and if the subject permitted I would have pleasure in narrating the campaign of the divisions under Lewis and Dunmore. But that would require a volume rather than an essay.* I shall content myself, therefore, with stating that the promised junction of Dunmore with Colonel Lewis was never effected. The earl changed his plan and descending the Ohio from Fort Pitt with a flotilla of one hundred canoes and several large boats to the mouth of the Hockhocking, erected a stockade which he called Fort Gower, and thence, ascended the Hockhocking to the falls near the present town of Athens. From that spot he crossed the country westward to the Scioto, and, on its eastern side, on the margin of the Piqua plains, near Scippo creek, entrenched himself in a regularly fortified camp, which, in honor of the British queen, he named Camp Charlotte.

* The following are the principal original authorities as to the campaigns and battles during the Dunmore war of 1774: 1. Col. Stuart's narrative in the *Virginia Historical and Philosophical Soc. Publications*, vol. I, Richmond, 1833, p. 35. 2. *Introduction to the Hist, of the Colony and Ancient Dominion of Virginia* by Campbell. 3. Kercheval's *Hist, of the Valley of Virginia.* 4. Doddridge's *Notes on the Settlement and Indian Wars of the W. Part of Va. and Penna.* 5. A. S. Withers's *Chronicle of Border Warfare.* 6. *Am. Archives*, 4th series, vol. I, especially p. 1016, et seq. 7. Howe's *Hist. Coll. of Ohio.* 8. Day's *Hist. Coll. of Penna.* 9. Howe's *Hist. Coll. of Virginia.* 10. Chas. Whittlesey's *Discourse before the Hist, and Phil. Soc. of Ohio, 1840.* 11. Burk's *Hist, of Va.* 12. Drake's *Book of the Indians*, book v, p. 42, et seq. 13. *Map of the Ancient Shawanese towns on the Pickaway Plains, and of Camp Charlotte and Lewis's camp, Howe's Ohio Hist. Coll.*

On the 10th of October the great and decisive battle of the campaign was fought by Lewis at Point Pleasant, at the mouth of the Kanawha, and it is regarded by most historians, as one of the most sanguinary and well-fought conflicts in the annals of Indian warfare in the west. The Indians, under the celebrated Cornstalk, were repulsed with great slaughter, and fled precipitately across the Ohio to their towns, sixty miles up the Scioto. In the meantime, Dunmore had sent detachments from his head-quarters against different settlements on the neighboring waters, which were sacked and burned; and such had been the bloody character of the battle at Point Pleasant that the chiefs hastened to appeal for peace to Dunmore, before they could be again assailed by the relentless Lewis, who was advancing in pursuit. After repeated overtures and the destruction of several towns, Dunmore consented to an armistice preparatory to a treaty. And, finally, after the two divisions had nearly effected a junction, the council fire was lighted, the council held, and peace resolved on.

But at the concluding scene of this bloody drama, the American and Indian chiefs did not find of its most daring actors, a man whose name is not signalized anywhere *in open battle* in the records or legends of the time, who was not in the conflict at Point Pleasant,* but whose war-path and weapon were only traced along the bloody trail of private murder. Logan was absent. He was not satisfied. He had taken, perhaps, some thirty scalps, but the ghosts of his murdered relatives were scarcely appeased in the hunting fields of the spirit land. When the cause of his absence was demanded, it was replied that he was yet like a mad dog; his bristles had been up and were not yet quite fallen; but the good talks now going forward, might allay them." He said he was " a warrior, not a councilor, and would not come!"

* That Logan was not present at the battle of Point Pleasant, is manifest from a MS. letter from "Colonel Wm. Christian to Col. William Preston, at Botetourt," in which he says: under date of Smithfield, Tuesday the 8th November 1774 :

"Last Friday was two weeks, Logan a famous chief, went home with a little boy, a son of Roberts, on Holston, and two of Blackmore's negroes. He said he had taken them on the frontiers next the Cherokee country, and had killed, I think, either five or seven people."

From the date of this letter, Logan's return, with his prisoners (young Roberts, son of the Roberts in whose house he had left the bloody missive) and the two negroes — occurred on the 20th October, eleven days after the battle of Point Pleasant. Lewis's army left Point Pleasant to join Dunmore's on Tuesday, October 18th, and on the Monday evening following, which was October 24th, it encamped within seven miles of Dunmore's army. Logan had returned October 21st; and on Tuesday, October 25th, Lewis's army commenced its return to Point Pleasant, which it reached on the night of Friday, 28th October.

These dates are derived from Colonel Christian's letter, which it is necessary to give *in extenso.*

The continued absence of Logan unquestionably filled the mind of Lord Dunmore with concern as to the stability of any peace which might be made with the Shawanese without the presence of a man who had shown such alacrity and bloodthirsty resolution in the cruel game of private war.

Accordingly, John Gibson, the alleged father of the Indian woman's infant rescued at the Yellow Creek massacre, was dispatched by the earl to seek for Logan. If, as is probable, the murdered squaw was Logan's sister, no messenger could have been more appropriately selected.

He found Logan some miles off at a hut with several Indians; and, pretending, in the Indian fashion, that he had nothing in view, talked and drank with them until the savage touched his coat stealthily, and, beckoning him out of the house, led him into a solitary thicket, where sitting down on a log, he burst into tears and uttered some sentences of impassioned eloquence, which Gibson, immediately returning to the British camp, committed to paper. As soon as the envoy had reduced the message to writing, it was read aloud in the council; heard by the soldiers; and proves to be neither a speech, a message, nor a pledge of peace :

"I appeal to any white man to say if ever he entered Logan's cabin hungry and he gave him not meat; if ever he came cold and naked and he clothed him not? During the course of the last long and bloody war, Logan remained idle in his camp, an advocate for peace. Such was my love for the whites that my countrymen pointed as I passed and said: 'Logan is the friend of the white man!' I had even thought to have lived with you, but for the injuries of one man. Colonel Cresap, the last spring, in cold blood and unprovoked, murdered all the relations of Logan, not even sparing my women and children. There runs not a drop of my blood in the veins of any living creature. This called on me for revenge. I have sought it. I have killed many. I have fully glutted my vengeance. For my country, I rejoice at the beams of peace; but do not harbor a thought that mine is the joy of fear. Logan never felt fear. He will not turn on his heel to save his life. Who is there to mourn for Logan? Not one!"1

Thus the speech of Logan, which has been so long celebrated as the finest specimen of Indian eloquence, dwindles into a reported conversation with, or outburst from a blood-stained savage; excited perhaps, when he delivered it, as well by the cruelties he had committed as by liquor; false in its allegations as to Cresap; and, at last, after being conveyed to a camp, about six miles distant, in the memory of Gibson, written down, and read by proxy to the council of Lord Dunmore. Gibson, it is true, states in his testimony that he corrected Logan on the spot when he made the charge against Cresap, for he knew his innocence, but either the Indian did not withdraw it or the messenger felt himself compelled to deliver it as originally framed. It was untrue also as to the slaughter of all his relations, women and children; for, years after, his relatives and his wife survived, while, it is known, he never had any children. When it was read in camp, the frontier men knew it to be false as to Michael Cresap; but it only produced merriment in the crowd, which displeased the Maryland captain. George Rogers Clark, who was near him, exclaimed, that "he must be a *very* great man, as the Indians shouldered him with everything that had happened." The captain smiled and replied that "he had a great inclination to tomahawk Greathouse about the matter!"*

* See Clark's letter, appendix No. 1. Clark was then a captain by commission from Dunmore, dated May 2d, 1774.

It is time to drop the curtain on these tragic scenes. The Indian fight was over; peace was made with the savage Shawanese, but a more heartless war was about to occur with the Christian Briton.

Cresap returned to Maryland and spent the latter part of the autumn of 1774 and the succeeding winter in the repose of a domestic circle from which he had been so long estranged; but, in the early spring of 1775, he hired another band of young men, and repaired again to the Ohio to finish the work he commenced the year before. He did not stop at his old haunts, but descended to Kentucky where he made some improvements. Being ill, however, he soon left his workmen and departed for his home over the mountains in order to rest and recover his health. On his way across the Alleghany Mountains he was met by a faithful friend with a message stating that he had been appointed, by the Committee of Safety at Frederick, a captain to command one of the two rifle companies required from Maryland by a resolution of congress.

Experienced officers, and the very best men that could be procured, were demanded.

"When I communicated my business," says the messenger, in his artless narrative, "and announced his appointment, instead of becoming elated, he became pensive and solemn, as if his spirits were really depressed, or, as if he had a presentiment that this was his death warrant. He said he was in bad health, and his affairs in a deranged state, but that, nevertheless, as the committee had selected him, and as he understood from me, his father had pledged himself that he should accept of this appointment, he would go, let the consequences be what they might. He then directed me to proceed to the west side of the mountains, and publish to his old companions in arms, this, his intention; this I did, and, in a very short time, collected and brought to him at his residence in Old Town, about twenty-two as fine fellows as ever handled rifle, and most, if not all of them, completely equipped.

"The immense popularity of this *infamous Indian murderer,* will appear from the circumstance of more than twenty men marching voluntarily nearly one hundred miles, leaving their families and their all, merely from a message sent by a boy, to join the standard of their old captain, and that too, from the very country where, if his name was odious, it must be most odious, as being in the vicinity of those dreadful Indian murders."*

*Jacob's *Life of Cresap,* p. 97.

This was in June, 1775; and already in August, we find by the following extract from a letter to a gentleman in Philadelphia, dated at Fredericktown, Maryland, that the young revolutionary hero was prepared to take the field.*

* From McCurtin's journal, printed by the Seventy-six society, at Philadelphia, in 1857, edited by Mr. Thomas Balch, in the volume of *Papers relative chiefly to the Maryland Line, I extract the following relative to the movement of these Maryland troops towards Cambridge: "The 18th day of July our company set off from Fredericktown (Md.), and traveled a quick but long journey in the space of 22 days, containing nearly 550 miles."*

"Notwithstanding the urgency of my business, I have been detained three days in this place by an occurrence truly agreeable. I have had the happiness of seeing Captain Michael Cresap marching at the head of a formidable company of upwards of one hundred and thirty men from the mountains and backwoods, painted like Indians, armed with tomahawks and rifles, dressed in hunting shirts and moccasins, and though some of them had traveled near eight hundred miles from the banks of the Ohio, they seemed to walk light and easy, and not with less spirit than the first hour of their march. Health and vigor, after what they had undergone, declared them to be intimate with hardship and familiar with danger. Joy and satisfaction were visible in the crowd that met them. Had Lord North been present, and been assured that the brave leader could raise thousands of such like to defend his country, what think you, would not the hatchet and the block have intruded on his mind? I had an opportunity of attending the captain during his stay in town, and watched the behavior of his men, and the manner in which he treated them; for it seems that all who go out to war under him do not only pay the most willing obedience to him as their commander, but, in every instance of distress look up to him as their friend and father. A great part of his time was spent in listening to and relieving their wants, without any apparent sense of fatigue and trouble. When complaints were before him, he determined with kindness and spirit, and on every occasion condescended to please without losing his dignity.

"Yesterday the company was supplied with a small quantity of powder from the magazine, which wanted airing, and was not in good order for rifles; in the evening, however, they were drawn out to show the gentlemen of the town their dexterity at shooting. A clap-board with a mark the size of a dollar was put up; they began to fire off-hand, and the bystanders were surprised, few shots being made that were not close to or in the paper. When they had shot for a time in this way, some lay on their backs, some on their breast or side, others ran twenty or thirty steps, and firing, appeared to be equally certain of the mark. With this performance the company were more than satisfied when a young man took up the board in his hand, not by the end but by the side, and holding it up, his brother walked to the distance and very coolly shot into the white; laying down his rifle, he took the board and holding it as it was held before, the second brother shot as the first had done. By this exercise I was more astonished than pleased. But will you believe me when I tell you that one of the men took the board, and placing it between his legs, stood with his back to a tree, while another drove the center!

"What would a regular army of considerable strength in the forests of America do with one thousand of these men, who want nothing to preserve their health and courage but water from the spring, with a little parched corn, with what they may easily procure in hunting; and who, wrapped in their blankets, in the damp of night, would choose the shade of a tree for their covering and the earth for their bed."*

* *American Archives,* vol. Ill, p. 2, transferred from the *Pennsylvania Gazette,* of Aug. 16, 1775.

Although in bad health Captain Cresap proceeded to Boston with this first company of Maryland riflemen, and joined the American army under the command of General Washington in August. Admonished, however, by continued illness, and feeling perhaps some forebodings of his fate, he endeavored once more, after about three months' service, to reach his home among the mountains, but finding himself too sick to proceed he stopped in New York, where he died of fever, on the 18th of October, 1775, at the early age of thirty-three.* On the following day his remains, attended by a vast concourse of people, were buried with military honors in Trinity church-yard. Let us deepen and not deface the inscription on his humble and neglected grave!

*McCurtain's Journal of the siege of Boston in Md Line Papers, ut antea, p.26 states 18th October as date of death. Jacob, p.98 gives 5th Oct. as date. Compare Jacob's Life of Cresap, p.98 and the Maryland Journal on Wednesday, Nov. 1, 1775. In the latter there is a letter from New York, dated the 26th of October, giving an account of his death and burial. "New York, Oct. 26th, 1775. On the 12th instant arrived here on his return from the Provincial Camp, at Cambridge, and, on the 18th, departed this life, of a fever, in the 28th year of his age "(should be 83d) " Michael Cressop, Esqre, eldest son of Col. Thomas Cressop, of Potomack in Virginia. He was Captain of a Rifle company now in the Continental army before Boston. He served as a Captain, under the command of Lord Dunmore in the late expedition against the Indians, in which he eminently distinguished himself by his prudence, firmness and intrepidity as a brave officer; and, in the present contest between the parent state and the colonies, gave proofs of his attachment to the rights and liberties of his country. He has left a widow and four children to deplore the loss of a husband and father; and by his death his country is deprived of a worthy and esteemed citizen. His remains were interred the day following, in Trinity Church-yard, with military honors, attended by a vast concourse of people." The author of this historical essay made frequent but ineffectual efforts to find the grave of Captain Cresap. His inquiries of the church officials were equally without result. At length, on a visit to the church-yard of Trinity, on the 2d of June, 1860, he discovered the long neglected grave and grave-stone of the pioneer, immediately opposite the door of the north transept of the church. It is of sandstone, and, when last seen in 1865, was broken off near the ground and propped up! It bears this inscription, beneath the rude sculpture of a winged head: "In Memory Of Michael Cresap First Capt of the Rifle Battalions, And Son Of Col Thomas Cresap, Who Departed This Life October The 18, 1775."

It is needless to speculate as to what such a man might have become had he been spared during the war of the revolution. Some of those who engaged in it as subordinates to him retired at its conclusion with high commissions granted for services which no hardy warrior of the revolution was more capable of yielding to the cause of his country than Michael Cresap.

Let us return once more for a moment to the Indian who has pursued the fame of our Marylander like a blighting shadow. We left him, confessedly fond of the fire-water, in his conversations with the missionary Heckewelder, and tippling before he became eloquent with Gibson. His last years were melancholy indeed. He wandered from tribe to tribe, a solitary and lonely man. Dejected by loss of friends and decay of his people, he resorted constantly to the stimulus of strong drink to drown his sorrow.

On the 25th of July, 1775, Captain James Wood having been sent with a single companion to invite the western Indians to a treaty at Fort Pitt, encountered Logan and several other Mingoes who had lately been prisoners at that post. He found them all drunk and inquisitive as to his designs. To his appeal the savages made no definite reply, but represented the tribes as very angry. The wayfarers bivouacked near the Indian town, and about ten o'clock at night one of the savages stole into the camp and stamped upon the sleeper's head. Starting to his feet and arousing his companion, Wood and the interpreter found several Indians around them armed with knives and tomahawks. For a while the Americans seem to have pacified the red men, but as a friendly squaw apprized them that the savages meditated their death, they stole away for concealment in the recesses of the forest. When they returned again to the Indian town after daylight, Logan repeated the foul story of the murder of his "mother, sister, and all his relations" by the people of Virginia. By turns he wept and sang. Then he dwelt and gloated over the revenge he had taken for his wrongs; and, finally, he told Wood that several of his fellows, who had long been prisoners at Fort Pitt, desired to kill the American messengers, and demanded if the forester was afraid? "No," replied Wood, "we are but two lone men, sent to deliver the message we have given to the tribes. We are in your power; we have no means of defense, and you may kill us if you think proper!" "Then," exclaimed Logan, apparently confounded by their coolness and courage, "you shall not be hurt!"—nor were they, for the ambassadors departed unmolested to visit the Wyandotte towns.*

*L. C. Draper's MSS. Journal of Captain James Wood. Jacob's Cresap, p. 85. Am. Archives, 4th series, vol. III, p. 77. Mrs. W. C. Rives's Tales and Souvenirs, preface and p. 146.

We next hear of Logan in the autumn of 1778, when the famous pioneer, Simon Kenton, who was taken prisoner by the savages, spent two nights with his captors and Logan on the head waters of the Scioto.

"Well, young man," said Logan addressing Kenton, on the night of his arrival, "these chaps seem very mad with you." "Yes," replied Kenton, "they appear so." "But don't be disheartened," interrupted Logan, "I am a great chief; you are to go to Sandusky; they talk of burning you there; but I will send two runners tomorrow to speak good for you!" And so he did, for on the morrow, having detained the hostile party, he dispatched the promised envoys to Sandusky, though he made no report to Kenton of their success when they returned at nightfall. The runners, by Logan's orders, interceded with Captain Druyer, an influential British Indian agent at Sandusky, who with great difficulty ransomed the prisoner and saved him from the brutal sacrifice of the stake.*

*Draper's MSS. McDonald's Memoir of Kenton. McClung's Sketches of Western Adventure.

In the fall of 1779, Logan appears again to have cast aside his humanity, and is found at his old jaunts on the Holston, engaged in the savage employment of scalping, or at least of taking prisoners.* And, in June, 1780, when Captain Bird, of Detroit, with a large body of British regulars, Canadians and Indians, invaded Kentucky, captured Ruddell's and Martin's Stations, and carried off a large number of prisoners, Logan was one of the marauders. **

*MS. letter in Mr. Draper's collection. American Pioneer, vol. I, p. 359.
** Draper's MSS.

Our Indian hero must now have been well nigh fifty-five years of age, and it may be supposed that so restless and fitful a life of natural impetuosity and artificial stimulus was drawing near its close. But his checkered career of crime, passion and occasional humanity, with all its finer features obliterated by the habitual use of intoxicating drinks, was doomed to end tragically.

It was not long after the inroad of Bird's British myrmidons and Indian allies in 1780, that Logan, at an Indian council held at Detroit, became wildly drunk, and, in the midst of delirious passion, prostrated his wife by a sudden blow. She fell before him apparently dead. In a moment, the horrid deed partly sobered the savage, who, thinking he had killed her, fled precipitately lest the stern Indian penalty of blood for blood might befall him at the hand of some relative of the murdered woman. While traveling alone, and still confused by liquor and the fear of vengeance, he was suddenly overtaken in the wilderness between Detroit and Sandusky, by a troop of Indians with their squaws and children, in the midst of whom he recognized his nephew or cousin Tod-kah-dohs. Bewildered as he was, he imagined that a lawful avenger pursued him in the form of his relative—for the Indian rule permits a relation to perform the retributive act of revenge for murder,—and, rashly bursting forth in frantic passion, he exclaimed that the whole party should fall beneath his weapon. Tod-kah-dohs, seeing their danger, and observing that Logan was well armed, told his companions that their only safety was in getting the advantage of the desperate man by prompt action. But Logan was quite as alert as his adversary; yet, whilst leaping from his horse to execute his threat, Tod-kah-dohs leveled a shot gun within a few feet of the savage and killed him on the spot!*

* Tod-kah-dohs or The Searcher, originally from Conestoga, and *probably* a son of Logan's sister residing there; died about 1844, at the Cold Spring on the Alleghany Seneca reservation, nearly one hundred years old. He was better known as Captain Logan, and was either a *nephew or cousin* of the celebrated Indian. He left children, two of whom have been seen by Mr. Draper; so that, in spite of Logan's speech, *some* of his "blood" still *"ran"* in human veins, ninety years after the Yellow Creek tragedy. Logan's *wife* was a Shawanese woman. *She had no children by him*; recovered from the blow received from her husband, and returned to her people. The fact that Logan's wife was a Shawanese, tends to explain the historical fact that the survivors of Logan's band after the Yellow Creek massacre, were taken by the Shawanese to their town of Wakatomica, and why the Shawanese generally and the warriors of Wakatomica in particular, entered so feelingly into Logan's desire for revenge. This, too, will explain how it happened that the two men mentioned by Bledsoe (in a previous note), knew Logan in the Shawanese nation.

The substance of this narrative was given to me in MS. by Mr. Lyman C. Draper, who received it from Dah-gan-on-do or Captain Decker, as it was related to him by Tod-kah-dohs, who killed Logan. "Decker," says Mr. Draper "was a venerable Seneca Indian, and the best Indian chronicler I have met with. His narratives are generally sustained by other evidence, and never seem confused or improbable." A different version of Logan's death is given, also, in Howe's *Ohio Hist. Coll.*, p. 409, upon the authority of Good Hunter, an aged Mingo, who is said to have been his familiar acquaintance. In this account he is represented to have been sitting before a camp fire near Detroit in Michigan, with his blanket drawn over his head, his elbows resting on his knees and his head upon his hands, buried perhaps in liquor, sleep or maudlin meditation, when an Indian, whom he had offended, stole behind him and buried a tomahawk in his brains! See also Vigne's *Six Months in America*, Philadelphia, edition 1833, p. 30, for another and very romantic version of his death from the hand of the same relative. Capt. Decker—Dah-gan-on-do—had lived all his eventful life of over one hundred years on the Alleghany, and knew Logan personally.— *Draper MSS.* See, also, Appendix No. 3 of this work.

When Mr. Jefferson wrote his *Notes on Virginia* in the years 1781 and 1782, he was anxious to disprove the theory of Buffon, Raynal and others, that animal nature—whether in man or beast, native or adoptive, physical or moral—degenerated in America. Whilst treating of the aborigines, he desired to present a specimen of their intellectual powers; and, finding in a pocket book a memorandum, made in the year 1774, of the alleged speech of Logan, as taken down by him at that time from the lips of someone whom he did not recollect, he inserted it in his *Notes,* accompanied by a slender narrative of the events that called it forth.* He spoke of Cresap as "a man infamous for the many murders he had committed on those much injured people," and charged the cold-blooded murder of Logan's family upon the Marylander and his allies. In a future edition he modified but did not entirely withdraw this charge;** and careless writers and historians down to the present day have continued to regard the Indian's talk, as remembered and related by Gibson, as a genuine speech solemnly delivered in council, and reiterate its cruel assertions as to the innocent Cresap. Poetry, even, has dwelt sweetly on the theme. Logan seems to have been the original whence Campbell derived his conception of Outalissi,*** and he has paraphrased, in rhyme, the passionate outburst:

> "' Gainst Brant himself I went to battle forth:—
> Accursed Brant!—he left of all my tribe
> Nor man, nor child, nor thing of living birth !
> No! not the dog that watched my household hearth
> Escaped that night of death upon our plains!
> All perished — I, alone, am left on earth!
> To whom nor relative, nor blood remains, —
> No! not a kindred drop that runs in human veins!"

* Jeff. *Notes on Va.,* appendix iv, p. 30.
**Ibid.* Stone's *Life of Brant,* vol. I, p. 39.
*** Graham's *Hist. United States,* vol. IV, p. 341. Stone's *Life of Brant,* vol. II, p. 525. *Gertrude of Wyoming,* part 3d, stanza XVII.

In his *notes,* Campbell repeats the old Logan and Cresap story j but in late editions, he retracted the errors of this passage — *as against Brant.* Brant's son when in London, pointed out to the poet the slanders of his verses, yet he left those slanders in the text of his poem, though he qualified them in his notes. "The *name of Brant,* therefore," says .Campbell, "remains in my poem, a pure and declared character of fiction." Yet, a thousand read the poem while only one will find the antidote in the note. The bad fame of the dishonored Brant will go to posterity with the taint of crime imputed by the poet, as the name of Cresap was maligned from year to year by a morsel of mendacious eloquence.

Mr. Jefferson's illustration of aboriginal eloquence obtained probably greater currency than he expected. It has become incorporated with English literature. Indian error converted Cresap into a monster, but. I have striven to restore to his memory its true and meritorious manhood. Fancy transformed the savage Logan into a romantic myth; and it has been my task not only to reduce this myth to a man, but to paint him as he really was—bright, generous and gentle, in youth, but degraded by cruelty and intemperance beneath the scale of aboriginal birthright. Indian instincts, kindled, it is true, by personal wrongs and by the flame of the fire-water, blighted a nature, which, at its dawn, promised a noble career. He murdered white men for revenge—not as a chief in open battle, but on the secret war path— and he nearly murdered his wife, under the less plausible delirium of drunkenness. In his intercourse with our race Logan lost nothing but the few virtues of a savage, while he gained from civilization very little but its vices.

Gravestone of Capt. Cresap, in Trinity Churchyard, New York, opposite the door of the North Transept.

APPENDIX No. 1.

General George Rogers Clark's Letter concerning the Yellow Greek Massacre, and exculpating Captain Michael Cresap.

The following letters, from Dr. Samuel Brown to General G. Rogers Clark, and General Clark's reply to him, were published by me in 1851, in the Appendix to the first edition of this narrative. They were furnished to me by Mr. Lyman C. Draper— Gen. Clark's letter having been previously published by the late L. C. Bliss, Jr., of Louisville College, in the Louisville *Literary News Letter,* "as taken from the letter-book of Gen. Clark, in his own handwriting." After Mr. Bliss's death, many of the original MSS. of Gen. Clark came into Mr. Draper's possession, and the transcripts of Brown's and Clark's letters were made by him for me from the General's letter book.

Dr. Samuel Brown's first letter is now printed from my first edition of this essay, while General Clark's letter and Dr. Brown's letter transmitted to Mr. Jefferson are printed from authenticated transcripts of the originals, in the first volume of the fifth series of the *Jefferson Papers,* and deposited in the department of state at Washington. Dr. Samuel Brown was long a distinguished professor in Transylvania University.

Dr. Samuel Brown's Letter.

"Lexington, *May 15th,* 1798.

"Dear Sir:

"At the request of our mutual friend, Mr. Jefferson, I enclose you a letter of Mr. Luther Martin on the subject of the murder of Logan's family, together with a vindication of the account of that transaction as related in the *Notes on Virginia.* I am sorry that it has not been possible to procure, in this place, the Baltimore paper which contains Mr. Martin's first publication on this question. The charges there exhibited against Mr. Jefferson are much more specific and more virulent than they appear to be in the letter now forwarded to you. It is possible, however, that the whole of the correspondence may have come to your hands by some other route. At all events, I presume Mr. Jefferson's answer will sufficiently apprise you of the nature of the dispute, and bring to your recollection such facts and circumstances as will tend to elucidate the doubtful and obscure parts of that interesting story.

" I remember to have had some conversation with you respecting the affair when at your house, and although the variety and important nature of the events which your conversations suggested, have in some degree effaced from my memory that distinct recollection of this particular event which I ought to have, before I should attempt to communicate your account of it to Mr. Jefferson, yet still I am pretty certain that as you related the story, any mistakes that have crept into the *Notes on Virginia* are not attributable to Mr. Jefferson, but to Logan himself, or to those by whom his speech was originally published. I think you informed me that you were with Cresap at the time Logan's family was murdered; that Cresap was not the author of that massacre; that Logan actually delivered the speech as reported in the *Notes on Virginia.* The Memoirs you have written of your own adventures, probably contain a full statement of the circumstances which gave rise to the dispute. A transcript from those Memoirs, or a statement of the business by you from memory, would be highly satisfactory to Mr. Jefferson and all his friends, and I am sure would be decisive evidence in the mind of every man of candor and liberality.

"I feel, and I am confident you must feel, sensibly hurt at a charge which can, in any degree, disturb the repose, or sully the reputation of that truly great and excellent man. I know you respect and esteem him, and I am really happy in assuring you that his respect and regard for you are equally cordial and sincere: of this, his last letter to me contains the most ample assurances. For myself, sensible that I have little which could entitle me to your friendship, I shall endeavor by my willingness to serve you, to convince you that I am truly thankful for those attentions I have received from you. And I shall consider myself singularly fortunate, if in any respect, I can be the means of rendering you and Mr. Jefferson mutually useful to each other. To your country you both have already been, and have it always in your power to be singularly useful.

"Mr. Thruston will do me the favor of carrying this letter, and I hope you will find leisure to prepare an account of Logan's speech before his return. I could wish to transmit it to Philadelphia before congress rises, as it is possible the conveyance to Monticello will not be so safe.

"Do me the favor of presenting my most respectful compliments to the family, and be assured that I am,

"With sentiments of real respect,

"Yr. mo. obt.,
"Sam. Brown."

"Gen. George E. Clark,
    "Jefferson County, Ky."

General George Rogers Clark to Dr. Samuel Brown.

"June 11th, 1798.

"Sir

"Your letter was handed to me by Mr. Thruston, the Matter therein contained was new to me; I find myself hurt that Mr. Jefferson should have been attacked with so much Virulence on a Subject which I know he was not the Author of, but except a few Mistakes of Names of Persons & Places, the Story is substantially true; I was of the first and last of the active Officers who bore the Weight of that War, and on perusing some old Papers of that Date I find some Memoirs, but independent of them I have a perfect Recollection of every Transaction relative to Logan's Story. The Conduct of Cresap I am perfectly acquainted with, he was not the Author of that Murder, but a family of the Name of Greathouse.—But some Transactions that happened under the Conduct of Capt" Cresap a few Days previous to the Murder of Logan's Family gave him sufficient Ground to suppose it was Cresap who had done him the Injury; But to enable you fully to understand the subject of your Enquiry, I shall relate the Incidents that gave rise to Logan's Suspicions, and will enable Mr. Jefferson to do Justice to himself and the Cresap Family by being made fully acquainted with the Facts.

"Kentucky was explored in 1773; A Resolution was formed to make Settlements in the Spring following & the Mouth of the little Kenhawa was appointed the Place of general Rendezvous — in order to descend the River thence in a Body; Early in the Spring the Indians had done some Mischief. Reports from their Towns were alarming, which caused many to decline Meeting, and only eighty or ninety Men assembled at the Place of Rendezvous, where we lay some Days; a Small Party of Hunters which lay about ten Miles below us were fired on by the Indians whom the Hunters beat off and returned to our Camp; This and many other Circumstances led us to believe that the Indians were determined to make War; the whole of our Party was exasperated, and resolved not to be disappointed in their Project of forming a Settlement in Kentucky, as we had every necessary Store that could be thought of. An Indian Town called Horse-Head Bottom on the *Siotho* and nearest its mouth lay most in our way, we resolved to cross the Country & *Surprize* it; who was to Command was the question; there were but few among us who had experience in Indian Warfare, and they were such as we did not chuse to be commanded by. We knew of Cap,', Cresap being on the River about 15 Miles above us with some Hands settling a new Plantation and intending to follow us to Kentucky as soon as he had fixed his People, we also knew that he had had Experience in a former War. It was proposed & unanimously agreed on to send for him to Command the Party; A Messenger was dispatched and in half an Hour returned with Cresap; he had heard of our Resolution by some of his Hunters who had fallen in with those from our Camp, and had set out to come to us; We now thought our little Army (as we called it) compleat, and the Destruction of the Indian Town inevitable; A Council was call'd, and to our Astonishment our intended General was the Person who dissuaded us from the *Enterprize, alledging* that appearances were suspicious, but that there was no Certainty of a War, that if we made the Attempt proposed he had no doubt of *Sucess,* but that a War at any Rate would be the Result, that we should be blamed for it and perhaps justly; but that if we were determined to execute the Plan, he would lay aside all considerations, send for his People and Share our Fortunes; he was then asked what Measure he would recommend to us, his Answer was that we should return to Wheeling, a convenient Post to obtain Intelligence of what was going forward, that a few Weeks would determine the Matter, and as it was early in the Spring, if we should find that the Indians were not hostilely disposed we should have full Time to prosecute our intended Settlements in Kentucky; This Measure was *adopte'd,* in two Hours the whole Party was under way; As we ascended the River we met Killbuck an Indian Chief (Delaware) with a small Party; We had a long Conference but obtained very little satisfaction from him. — It was observed that Cresap did not attend this Conference but kept on the Opposite side of the River, he Said that he was afraid to trust himself with the Indians; that Killbuck had frequently attempted to waylay & kill his Father, & that he was Doubtful that he should be tempted to put Killbuck to Death.—On our arrival at Wheeling, the whole Country being pretty well settled thereabouts, the Inhabitants appeared to be much alarmed, and lied to our Camp from every Direction.—We offered to Cover their *Neighbourhood* with Scouts, until we could obtain further Information, if they would return to their Plantations; but Nothing we could say would prevail; By this Time we got to be a formidable Party as all the Hunters & Men without Families &c in that quarter joined us. Our Arrival at Wheeling was known at Pittsburgh, the whole of that Country at that time being under the Jurisdiction of Virginia. Dr. Connelly had been appointed by Dunmore Capt Commandant of the District then Called West Augusta; He Connelly hearing of us sent a Message addressed to the Party, informing us that a War was to be apprehended, and requesting that we would keep our Position for a few Days, that Messengers had been sent to the Indian Towns whose return he daily expected, and the Doubt respecting a War with the Indians would then he cleared up. — The Answer we returned was that we had no Inclination to decamp for some Time, and during our stay we should be Careful that the Enemy should not *harrass* the *Neighbourhood*. — But before this Answer could reach Pittsburgh he had sent a second Express addressed to Capt. Cresap as the most influential Man amongst us informing him that the Messengers had returned from the Indian Towns and that a War was inevitable, and *begg'd* him to use his Influence with the Party to get them to Cover the Country until the Inhabitants could fortify themselves. — The Time of the Reception of this Letter was the Epoch of open Hostilities with the Indians. The War Post was planted, a Council Called and the Letter read and the Ceremonies used by the Indians on so important an Occasion acted, and War was formally declared. — The same evening two scalps were brought into Camp. — The following Day some Canoes of Indians were discovered descending the River, taking advantage of an Island to cover themselves from our View. They were chased by our Men 15 Miles down the River, they were forced ashore and a Battle ensued, a few were wounded on both sides and we got one scalp only; On examining their Canoes we found a considerable quantity of ammunition and other Warlike Stores. On our return to Camp a Resolution was formed to march next Day and attack Logan's Camp, on the Ohio, about 30 Miles above Wheeling. We actually marched about five Miles, and halted to take some Refreshment, here the Impropriety of executing the proposed *Enterprize* was argued, the Conversation was brought forward by Cresap himself; it was generally agreed that those Indians had no hostile Intentions, as it was a hunting Camp composed of Men Women and Children with all their Stuff with them. This we knew as I myself and others then present had been at their Camp about four weeks before that time on our way down from Pittsburgh; In short every Person present particularly Cresap (upon Reflection) was opposed to the projected Measure. We returned & on the same evening Decamped and took the Road to Red-Stone. — It was two Days after this that Logan's Family was killed, and from the Manner in which it was done, it was viewed as a horrid Murder by the whole Country. From Logan's hearing that Cresap was at the Head of the Party at Wheeling it was no wonder that he considered Cresap as the Author of his Family's Destruction.

"Since the Receipt of your Letter I have procured the Notes on Virginia, they are now before me; the Action was more barbarous than therein related by Mr. Jefferson; those Indians used to visit & receive Visits from the *neighbouring* Whites on the Opposite Shore,, they were on a Visit at *Greathouse's* at the Time they were *massacre'd* by those People and their associates. The War now raged with all its Savage Fury until the following fall, when a Treaty of Peace was held at Dunmore's Camp within five Miles of Chilicothe, the Indian Capital on the *Siotho*. — Logan did not appear — I was acquainted with him & wished to he informed of the Reason of his absence by one of the Interpreters. The Answer he gave to my Enquiry was "that he was like a Mad Dog, that his Bristles had been up and were not yet quite fallen — but that the good Talks now going forward might allay them."—Logan's Speech to Dunmore now came forward as related by Mr. Jefferson, and was generally believed & indeed not doubted to have been genuine and dictated by Logan. — The Army knew it was wrong so far as it respected Cresap and afforded an Opportunity of rallying that Gentleman on the subject. — I discovered that Cresap was displeased and told him that he must be a very great Man that the Indians shouldered him with every Thing that had happened — he smiled & said he had a great mind to tomahawk Greathouse about the matter. — What is here related is Fact, I was intimate with Cresap, and better acquainted with Logan at that Time than with any other Indian in the Western Country, and had Knowledge of the Conduct of both Parties. Logan is the Author of the Speech as related by Mr. Jefferson, and Cresap's Conduct was such as I have related.

"I have gone through a Relation of Every Circumstance that had any Connection with the Information you desire & hope it will be satisfactory to yourself & Mr. Jefferson.

"I am your mo. *obt,* serv

G. R. Clark."

"Doc. Sam. Brown."

Dr. Samuel Brown to Mr. Jefferson, transmitting General Clark's Letter.

Lexington, Ky., *4th Sept.* 1798.

"Dear Sir,

"The letter you did me the honor of writing me in March last, I intended to have answered long since; and, to enable me to do so the more to your satisfaction, I took the earliest opportunities of informing General Clark, and several other gentlemen who had been the companions of his youthful campaigns, of the illiberal attack made on you by the attorney general of Maryland. I have deferred replying to your friendly letter hitherto from an expectation of collecting from different sources a variety of statements and facts relative to the murder of Logan's family. But, as mo3t of the gentlemen to whom I wrote on the subject, reside in remote parts of the country, at a distance from post roads, I am induced to attribute their silence to the want of safe modes of conveying their letters to Lexington. I am happy, however, in having it in my power to transmit to you an interesting letter from your friend General Clark, which indeed appears to me to render further investigation quite unnecessary. The only point for which you contend, viz: that Logan is really the author of the speech ascribed to him in your *Notes on Virginia* is now established beyond the possibility of contradiction. The incidents in General Clark's narrative follow each other in a manner so simple and so natural as to afford to every liberal and candid inquirer the highest internal evidence of their reality. To those who have the happiness of being acquainted with that truly great man, his statement will bring the fullest conviction. His memory is singularly accurate, his veracity unquestionable. To such respectable authority, I can suppose no one capable of objecting, except Mr. Luther Martin.

"I have shown General Clark's letter to Major Morrison* the supervisor of the Ohio district, who resided near Pittsburgh where the transactions respecting Logan occurred. He assures me that he knows most of them as stated in the letter to be true, for they are within his own recollection.

* Major James Morrison was an officer in Colonel D. Brodhead's Penn. regiment, long stationed at Pittsburgh, during the revolution, and afterwards became a prominent citizen of Lexington, Ky. He was a supervisor of the United States revenue.

Colonel Paterson,* who likewise lived in that country about that time, mentioned to me a circumstance which appears worthy of notice. There were then on that, as on almost every other frontier, two parties. By the one, Captain Cresap was considered as a wanton violator of treaties, as a man of a cruel, inhuman disposition—by the other, he was esteemed as an intrepid warrior, and a just avenger of savage barbarities. You probably, became first acquainted with his character at Williamsburg, the seat of government; General Clark joined him in the war-path. This circumstance will, perhaps, in some measure, account for the very different sentiments which two gentlemen so perfectly capable of appreciating Cresap's character, may have entertained respecting it.

*Colonel Robert Paterson was an early, meritorious pioneer of Kentucky; afterwards settled at Dayton, Ohio, where he died in 1827. He was a perfectly reliable man.

"Should you judge it advisable at the present time, I could easily obtain from General Clark the substance of his narrative, and have it published here, as an answer to spontaneous inquiries of my own. It can be done without you appearing at all in the business. This, however, I shall not attempt to do without your permission; yet, I wish that General Clark's statement could be made public in some shape or other as it would doubly mortify Mr. Martin to hear his assertions refuted without receiving a reply from you whom he has so assiduously labored to draw forth into the field of controversy.

"I can assure you that your friends in this quarter are highly gratified at the silent contempt with which you have treated that redoubtable hero of Federalism. And it is with heartfelt pleasure that I further assure you that nothing which old Tories, aristocrats, and governmental sycophants can say against you, will in any degree, diminish the confidence which the good citizens of this state repose in your abilities and patriotism.

> "With sincerest wishes &c.
> "Samuel Brown.

"To Hon. Thos. Jefferson."

The omitted end of the letter is about irrelevant matters.

The accuracy of the preceding two letters is attested by the following certificate annexed to them:

> "United States Of America
> "Department *of State.*

"To all to whom these presents shall come, greeting: "I certify that annexed is a true copy of an Original letter from G. R. Clark to Dr. Samuel Brown, dated June, 17, 1798, and one from Dr. Samuel Brown to Thomas Jefferson, dated September 4th, 1798, both found among the Jefferson papers deposited in this Department.

" In testimony whereof, I, "William H. Seward, Secretary of State of the United States, have hereunto subscribed my name and caused the seal of the Department of [L.S.] State to be affixed. Done at the city of Washington this eighth day of April, A. D. 1867, and of the Independence of the United States of America the Ninety first."

"Signed,
"William H. Seward."

This correspondence shows that Mr. Jefferson was annoyed by the bitter strictures that were made by the Hon. Luther Martin *who had married Michael Cresap's daughter,* and which were called forth in vindication of his father-in-law, by the original version of the captain's conduct in 1774 as given on page 91 of the edition of the *Notes on Virginia,* published by Matthew Carey at Philadelphia, in 1794. In 1797 and 1798 Mr. Jefferson was preparing his vindication, as will appear by the dates of Mr. Martin's communication to Fennell on the 29th of March, 1797, and Jefferson's letters to John Gibson in February, 1798, and in March, 1800 (republished in the *Olden Time Magazine* for February, 1847), also of the Appendix No. iv to his *Notes on Virginia,* and the affidavits comprised in it, as published in the 1800 edition. At that time Mr. Jefferson, it will be recollected, was the head of the *Democratic* party in the country, while Luther Martin was an eminent leader of the *Federalists.* Party feelings and party animosities were bitter. It is very probable that such feelings were mingled, on both sides, in the controversy on the Logan and Cresap story. At all events, Jefferson was a long time obtaining his testimony from Gibson, beginning his request, apparently in February, 1798, and not getting the affidavit until two years after, on the 4th of April, 1800, and then under the allurement of a long and singular letter which is given at length in the *Olden Time,* volume II, page 55.

I may properly add here that I have a MS. copy of an affidavit of Mr. John Caldwell, who resided near Wheeling in 1774, which fully exonerates Cresap from all participation in the murder of Logan's family.

The following is the text of Mr. Caldwell's affidavit taken in the year 1839.

He states: "That in the year 1774, he emigrated from Baltimore, Md., to the western country, and settled at the mouth of Wheeling creek, on the Ohio, in what was known as the district of West Augusta, and afterwards and now as Ohio County, Virginia. That he was well and intimately acquainted with the late Captain Michael Cresap, of Frederick County, Md., in 1774, and for some time before, and afterwards till his death. At the time last mentioned, the section of country in which affiant resided was frequently disturbed by the Indians (as well for several years previous to 1774, as for many years afterwards), who were in the habit of stealing horses from the white inhabitants on the frontier, and committing other depredations. Horses were stolen from Wm. McMahon and Jos. Tomlinson and others in 1774. Much ill feeling at all times existed among the white people of the frontier against the Indians on account of their depredations and the murders which they had at different times committed among the settlements. In 1774, several Indians who had dwelt on the west side of the Ohio, at or near the mouth of Yellow Creek, crossed over the river to what was then known as Baker's Bottom, opposite or nearly opposite the mouth of said creek, and were killed by the whites at that place, as the affiant always understood and well believes, from feelings of animosity growing out of the causes aforesaid against the Indians generally. The Indians so killed were said to have been, and affiant believes such was the fact, the relatives or family of the chief, Logan, with whose massacre the said Captain Cresap is charged in Jefferson's *Notes on Virginia,* Dr. Doddridge's *Notes,* etc. At the time said Indians were killed, Captain Cresap made his home at the house of affiant, at the mouth of Wheeling creek, but was generally absent, further down the river, with a party of men in his employ, making improvements on lands he had taken up near Middle Island creek. Shortly before, and at the time of the massacre of Logan's relatives, there was a general apprehension on the frontiers from various indications, that there was to be a general out-breaking of the Indians upon the settlements, and much alarm prevailed. Captain Cresap and his men came up the river to affiant's house, and affiant well remembers that he, Captain Cresap, was there on the day the Indians referred to were killed at Baker's Bottom, and that he remained there for some days afterwards and until the news of their being killed reached Wheeling. Affiant further states that Baker's Bottom was situated forty or fifty miles above his residence, immediately on the Ohio River: that on the evening of the day the report reached Wheeling, that the Indians had been killed, affiant started down the river to Middle-Island Creek, where he, also, had some hands engaged in making improvements, to warn them of the danger apprehended by the people above, and to bring them home; and that when he left home, Captain Cresap was at his house.

"*Affiant further states that he was called on, some years ago, by some person, whose name he does not now remember, but who was understood to be the agent or as acting under the direction of Mr. Jefferson, for his, affiant's, testimony in relation to the murder of Logan's family, and that he then gave his affidavit, which, in substance, was the same as the foregoing.* Affiant further says it was well understood and believed on the frontier at that time that the persons principally engaged in killing said Indians were Daniel (John?)

Sappington, Nathaniel Tomlinson, Daniel Greathouse, and perhaps, others; and that Captain Cresap was never charged or implicated in the report, in any manner, so far as he knows or believes, in this country, until after the publication of Jefferson's *Notes on Virginia.'"*

Mr. John Caldwell, who made this affidavit, is represented to have been a gentleman of irreproachable character, brother of the late Alexander Caldwell, long a judge of the United States court for the western district of Virginia. The affidavit was reduced to writing by Mr. Daniel M. Edgington, a lawyer of Wheeling, W. Virginia, in 1839.

APPENDIX No. 2

Logan's Speech

I have thought that it would interest many readers if I grouped together in an appendix the evidence that has been adduced both for and against Logan's message or speech, and, at the same time, presented, side by side, such exact copies of this document, as I have been enabled to discover from the earliest dates. Importance was given to the article, as we have already seen, by the illustrative use made of it by Mr. Jefferson, as well as by its intrinsic merit.

FOR THE SPEECH

The first piece of testimony in favor of the *message* from Logan, comes from John Gibson, and was sworn to and subscribed by him before J. Barker, at Pittsburgh, Pa., on the 4th of April, 1800, *twenty-six years* after the event occurred:

I. This deponent being duly sworn said: That in the year 1714, he accompanied Lord Dunmore on the expedition against the Shawanese and other Indians on the Scioto; that on their arrival within *fifteen miles* of the towns they were met by a flag and a *white man* by the name of Elliot, who informed Lord Dunmore that the Chiefs of the Shawanese had sent to request his lordship to *halt his army and send in* some person who understood their language; that this deponent, *at the request of Lord Dunmore, and the whole of the officers with him,* went in; that on his arrival at the towns, Logan, the Indian, came to where this deponent was sitting with the Cornstalk, and the other chiefs of the Shawanese, and asked him to walk out with him; that they went into a copse of wood where they sat down, when Logan, after shedding abundance of tears, delivered to him the speech, *nearly as related by Mr. Jefferson in his Notes on the State of Virginia ;* that he the deponent, *told him then that it was not* Colonel Cresap *who had murdered his relatives,* and although *his son,* Captain Michael Cresap, was *with* the party who had killed a *Shawanese* chief and *other* Indians, yet he was not present when his Relatives were killed at Baker's, near the mouth of Yellow Creek, on the Ohio;— that this deponent, *on his return to camp, delivered the speech to Lord Dunmore;* and that the murders perpetrated as above *were considered* as ultimately the cause of the war of 1774, commonly called Cresap's War.

Signed: John Gibson.

II. Genl. George Rogers Clark says, in his letter of the 17th June, 1798 (ut antea), *twenty-four years after the event,* that when the treaty was holding at Camp Charlotte, within *four* (?) miles of Chillicothe, the *Indian* capital of Ohio, Logan did not appear. "I was acquainted with him, and wished to know the reason. The answer was: that he was like a mad dog: his bristles had been up, and were not yet quite fallen; but the good talk now going forward might allay them.' *Logan's speech to Dunmore, as related by Mr. Jefferson, now came forward. It was thought clever though the army knew it to be wrong as to Cresap. But it only produced a laugh in the camp. I saw it displeased Capt. Cresap, and told him, that he must be a very great man; that the Indians had palmed everything that happened on his shoulders. He smiled, and said that he "had an inclination to tomahawk Greathouse for the murder."*

III. My late friend James Dunlof, counselor at law, in Pittsburgh, since dead, wrote to me, under date of April 25th, 1851, as follows:

"I am well informed that Colonel Gibson, who was an uncle of Chief Justice Gibson, has frequently repeated here the story of Logan's delivering the speech to him. He used to say that at the treaty Lord Dunmore was about to hold with the Shawanese, he was uneasy at the absence of so distinguished a chieftain as Logan, and being indisposed to proceed without his presence, sent Col. Gibson for him; that he, Col. Gibson, found him some miles off at a hut with several other Indians; that pretending in the Indian way, that he had nothing in view, he walked about, talked, and drank with them until Logan pulled him quietly by the coat, and calling him out, took him some distance into a solitary thicket, where, sitting down on a log, the Indian burst into tears and broke out in the impassioned language which glows so eloquently in the *speech.* Gibson said that he *returned at once to his friends and wrote down* the language of Logan immediately, and delivered it to Lord Dunmore in Council."

IV. The message or speech was circulated freely at Williamsburgh immediately after Dunmore's return from his campaign in the winter of 1774, and was *published* then in the *Virginia Gazette* on the 4th

February, 1775, and in New York on the 16th Feb., 1775, as will be seen hereafter.

V. William McKee testifies in the IVth Appendix to Jefferson's *Notes on Va.,* p. 42, that being in the camp on *the evening* of the treaty made by Dunmore with the Indians, he heard "*repeated conversations* concerning an *extraordinary speech made* at the treaty, *or sent* there by a chieftain of the Indians named Logan, and *heard several attempts at a rehearsal of it*" &c., &c. See also Andrew Rodgers's certificate as to these facts in the same Appendix, p. 44.

AGAINST THE SPEECH

I. See an argument on this subject written by the Hon. Luther Martin, son-in-law of Capt. Michael Cresap, and formerly a distinguished counselor at law and attorney general of the state of Maryland, in which he attempts to impugn this speech. It is dated the 29th March, 1197; and is addressed to Mr. James Fennell, who in his public readings as an elocutionist had given force and currency to the Logan speech.

This letter republished in the *Olden Time Magazine,* vol. II, p. 51, drew forth the argumentative vindication, contained in Mr. Jefferson's IVth Appendix to his *Notes on Virginia* to which so many references have been made in the course of this narrative.

II. Withers in his *Chronicles of Border Warfare,* p. 186, says, "Two *interpreters* were sent to Logan by Lord Dunmore, requesting his attendance; but Logan replied, that he was a warrior, not a counselor and would not come!

In a note on this passage, Mr. Withers adds: "Colonel Benjamin Wilson, Senr.," then an officer in Dunmore's army, says "that he conversed freely with one of the interpreters (Nicholson) in regard to the mission to Logan, and that neither from the interpreter, nor from any other one during the campaign, did he hear of the charge preferred in Logan's speech against Capt. Cresap as being engaged in the affair at Yellow Creek. Capt. Cresap was an officer *in the division under Lord Dunmore;* and it would seem strange, indeed, if Logan's speech had been made public at Camp Charlotte, and neither he (who was so naturally interested in it, and could at once have proven the falsehood of the allegation it contained), nor Colonel Wilson (who was present during the whole conference between Lord Dunmore and the Indian chiefs, and at the time when the speeches were delivered, sat immediately behind and close to Dunmore), *should have heard nothing of it until years after"*

III. Mr. Neville B. Craig, in the 2d vol. of his *Olden Time Magazine,* page 54, published at Pittsburgh in 1847, when discussing the authenticity of the speech, says: "We will state, that many years ago, Mr. James McKee, the brother of Alex. McKee, the deputy of Sir William Johnson, stated to us distinctly, *that he had seen the speech in the handwriting of one of the Johnsons,* whether Sir William or his successor, Guy, we do not recollect, before it WAS SEEN BY LOGAN!

The reader will also find arguments by Mr. Craig against the authenticity of the speech in this 2d vol. of the *Olden Time Magazine,* at pages 49 and 475.

IV. Jacob in his *Life of Cresap* gives the testimony of Mr. Benjamin Tomlinson, on page 106 of his work. This testimony was prepared in Cumberland, Md., April 17, 1797, *twenty-three years* after the occurrence of the events.

The testimony is given by question and answer:

Question 6th; Was Logan at the treaty held by Dunmore with the Indians at Camp Charlotte, on Scioto? Did he make a speech, and, if not, who made it for him?

"*Answer;* To this question I answer— Logan was not at the treaty. Perhaps Cornstalk, the chief of the Shawanese nation, mentioned among other grievances, the Indians killed on Yellow Creek but I *believe* neither Cresap nor any other person, were named as the perpetrators; and I perfectly recollect that I was that day officer of the guard, and stood near Dunmore's person, that consequently I saw and heard all that passed; — that, also, *two or three days before* the treaty, when I was on the out-guard, Simon Girty, who was passing by, stopped with me and conversed; he said he was going after Logan, but he did not like the business, for he was a surly fellow; he, however, proceeded on, and I saw him return on the day of the treaty, and Logan was not with him; at this time a circle was formed and the treaty begun ; I saw John Gibson, on Girty's arrival, get up and go out of the circle and talk with Girty, after which he (Gibson) went into a tent, and soon after returning into the circle, drew out of his pocket a piece of clean new paper, on which was written in his own hand-writing — a speech for and in the name of Logan. This I heard read three times, once by Gibson, and twice by Dunmore the purport of which was that he, Logan, was the white man's friend, that on his journey to Pittsburgh to brighten this friendship, or on his return thence, all his friends were killed at Yellow Creek; that now when he died, who should bury him, for the blood of Logan was running in no creatures' veins; *but neither was the name of Cresap, or the name of any other person mentioned in this speech.** But I recollect to see Dunmore put this speech among the other treaty papers."

* This would make it *correspond* with the Abbe Robin's copy, which follows in this volume.

From these parallel statements it will be seen that the chief evidence against the authenticity of the speech or message as detailed by John Gibson, is given by Col. Wilson, and by Mr. Tomlinson who was a citizen of our state, residing in Alleghany County, and admitted to be a person of respectable character for truth and intelligence. Testimony to this effect is adduced from high sources, and published in the 2d vol. of the *Olden Time Magazine,* page 476.

A sketch of John Gibson will be found in T. J. Rogers's *American Biographical Dictionary,* 4th edition, Philadelphia, 1829. He has always been regarded as an honest and truthful person. He enjoyed the confidence of Washington who, in 1781 entrusted him with the command of the Western Military department. In 1782, when Gen. Irvine had succeeded him, Gibson was entrusted with the command during the general's absence, which continued for several months. Jefferson, Madison and Harrison respected him. He was a major general of militia, secretary of Indian territory under the administration of Jefferson and Madison; member of the Pennsylvania convention in 1778; and an associate judge of the court of common pleas of Alleghany County, Pa. Chief Justice Gibson and General George Gibson, sons of Col. George Gibson, who was mortally wounded at St. Clair's defeat, are his well known and esteemed nephews.

It will be observed that Mr. Tomlinson does not allege that Gibson did *not* go to Logan's village. He makes no statement in regard to him, until he saw him in the camp with Girty. And yet, it may have been perfectly consistent with the facts as they occurred, that Gibson visited the Indian villages without Mr. Tomlinson being aware of his absence. Nothing was more likely to occur in a frontier camp. It is possible that Girty may have accompanied Gibson, as both had, many years before been Indian captives and were well acquainted with the Shawanese and Mingoes. Gibson says, according to Mr. Dunlop's statement, that Logan's message was not reduced to writing until his return to camp; and if Girty accompanied him, nothing was so probable as that they should unite and resort to a tent to commit it to paper. General Clark's letter seems to prove, conclusively, that Cresap's *name was* in the message when read in the camp, for he jeered him with his asserted importance in originating the war, whereupon Cresap broke forth in bitter invective against Greathouse; and, moreover, it is evident that Logan had previously charged Cresap with the murder, as will be seen by reference to the note addressed to *"Captain Cresap"* which the Indian left in the house of Roberts, whose family he had murdered in 1774.

I think it may be fairly deduced from the preceding statements, that John Gibson, in his interview with Logan, heard from him an outburst of passionate sorrow, the purport of which *he subsequently reduced to writing after his return to the British camp from the Indian villages, a distance of about six miles.* When he reached camp, in all likelihood, he detailed the conversation with Logan to Lord Dunmore; and the Earl and the Indian trader, who were both anxious to make Logan participate in the treaty in some manner, committed the remembered language of the savage to paper, and caused it to be read forthwith to the army as a *speech or message* from Logan. The reader will not fail to remark, that *intrinsically, it does not pretend in its language to be a message, a speech or a pledge for the future; and, when critically examined, is nothing more than a savage expostulation or apology for cruelties committed by a man of strong feelings, but in which not a single note of personal grief or of submission is mingled.*

* See Howe's *Ohio Hist. Collections*, p. 402, for a Map of the Ancient Shawanese Towns on the Pickaway Plains, made by P. N. White, and containing the sites of Logan's cabin, Camp Charlotte (Dunmore's), and the position of Lewis's division when halted by the earl. This map shows that the distance between Logan's cabin and Dunmore's head-quarters *was fully, six miles.*

In all the versions of this paper which I am about to present, there is no *consent by Logan to the peace,* except in the copy given by the Abbe Robin; and if Dunmore wanted Logan's adhesion to the treaty, *that* speech would most probably have satisfied him. The *French copy* it will be observed, does not contain the name of Cresap.

Different Versions of the Speech.

I have diligently sought for the early copies of this celebrated document, which are known to exist in our country, and the following are the fruits of my researches. The first is taken from a work which I found in the Maryland Historical Society's collection. It is entitled: *Nouveau Voyage dans L'Amerique seplentrionale, en l'Annee* 1781; *et Compagne de VArmee de M. le Comte de Eochambeau, par M. Vabbi Robin."* The abbe was a chaplain in the army of our French auxiliaries:

Original French or The Abbe Robin, PUBLISHED IN PHILADELPHIA And Paris In 1782.

I.

ORIGINAL FRENCH OF THE ABBÉ RO-
BIN, PUBLISHED IN PHILADELPHIA
AND PARIS IN 1782.

II.

TRANSLATION, PUBLISHED AT PHILA-
DELPHIA IN 1783.

"On a reproché aux Espagnols leurs cruautés contre ceux des pays dont ils se sont emparés : il paroit qu'on auroit aussi des reproches de ce genre à faire aux Colonies Angloises. Ce discours que m'a communiqué un professeur de Williamsburgh, dont voici la traduction, en est un monument. Ill montre, en même temps, avec quelle mâle énergie ces sauvages savent s'exprimer :

" The Spaniards have been reproached for exercising cruelties upon the inhabitants of the countries they conquered ; but it appears that reproaches of this kind are no less well founded against the English. An Indian speech that was given me by a professor at Williamsburgh, a translation of which is subjoined, is a proof of this. It discovers, at the same time, the bold and masculine energy these savages are taught by nature to express themselves :

" DISCOURS PRONONCE PAR LE SAUVAGE LONAN, DANS UNE ASSEMBLEE GENERALE, ENVOYE A M. le GOUVERNEUR DE VIRGINIE, LE 11 NET¹ 1754 :

"SPEECH PRONOUNCED BY THE SAVAGE LONAN, IN A GENERAL ASSEMBLY AS IT WAS SENT TO THE GOVERNOR OF VIRGINIA, ANNO 1754 :

" LONAN ne s'opposera jamais à faire la paix qu'on propose avec les Hommes blancs. Vous savez qu'il ne connut jamais la crainte, et qu'il n'a jamais fui dans les combats. Personne n'aime plus que moi les Hommes blancs. La guerre que nous venons d'avoir avec eux, a été longue et cruelle des deux côtés. Des ruisseaux de sang out coulé de toutes parts, sans qu'il en soit résulté aucun bien pour personne. Je le répete, faisons la paix avec ces hommes ; j'oublie leurs injures, l'intèrêt de mon pays l'exige : j'oublie encore que, naguere, le Major ———, fit massacrer impitoyablement, dans un bateau, ma femme, mes enfens, mon père, ma mère, et tous mes parens. L'on m'excita à la vengence — je fus cruel malgré moi. Je mourrai content si ma patrie est en paix : mais quand Lonan ne sera plus, qui est-ce qui versera pour lui une larme ? " 2

"Lonan will no longer oppose making the proposed peace with the white man — you are sensible that he never knew what fear is — that he never turned his back in the day of battle — no one has more love for the white man than I have. The war we have had with them has been long and bloody on both sides — rivers of blood have run on all parts, and yet no good has resulted therefrom to any. I once more repeat it — let us be at peace with these men ; I will forget our injuries, the interest of our country demands it — I will forget, but difficult indeed is the task — yes, I will forget, Major *Rogers cruelly and inhumanly murdered in their canoes, my wife, my children, my father, my mother, and all my kindred.* This roused me to deeds of vengeance — I was cruel in despight of myself — I will die content if my country is once more at peace : but when Lonan shall be no more who alas ! will drop a tear for him." 3

The speech translated from the Abbe Robin's work is tolerably well rendered into English by the translator at Philadelphia in 1783, though it is not as accurate or neat as it might be. The main facts, however, are faithfully given, and we cannot doubt that it is the speech or message usually attributed to *Logan,* though it is assigned to *Logan,* and that the date of 1754 for 1774 was a misprint or an inaccuracy either of the professor at Williamsburgh, or of the Abbe in translating the original into French. The date, in the French copy of "11 *Net,"* is probably also a misprint for 11th November, inasmuch as the treaty having been made by Dunmore near the close of October, 1774, this copy of the speech may very probably have been committed to writing and got abroad early in the following November. The general cast of thought in the speeches reported by Jefferson and the Abbe is the same; but they differ in force, elegance and eloquence. The essential points, however, to which I desire to call the reader's attention are: that in the French edition the massacre is attributed, not to Cresap, but to a "Major;" in the English translation the blank is filled by the name of "Major *Rogers"* and finally that Logan or Lonan asserts this bloodthirsty commander murdered *his wife,* his *children,* his *father,* his *mother,* and *all his kindred,* In THEIR CANOE.

Now, it will be recollected that Shikellamy, his father, died at Shamokin in 1749; so that he could not have been killed at Yellow Creek in 1774; and, moreover, that Mr. Jefferson, in his *Notes on Virginia* (edition of 1794) says that "Col. Cresap, a man infamous for the many murders he had committed on these much injured people, collected a party and proceeded *down the Kanawha* in quest of vengeance. Unfortunately a canoe *of women and children with one man only,* was seen coming from the opposite shore, unarmed and unsuspecting a hostile attack from the whites. Cresap and his party concealed themselves on the bank of the river, and the moment the canoe reached the shore, singled out their objects, and, at one fire, killed every person in it. This happened to be *the family of Logan* who had long been distinguished as a friend of the whites."

Here the story of the murder *in canoes* and of the whole of Logan's family was repeated, and the geography of the scene is ascribed to the Kanawha. This, upon examination, was found by Mr. Jefferson to be inaccurate, and in the edition of the *Notes on Virginia,* which he retained by him until his death, and in the IVth appendix to more recent editions than that of 1794, he caused the paragraph above cited to be substituted by the following:

"Capt. Michael Cresap and a certain Daniel Greathouse, leading on these parties, surprised at different times, travelling and hunting parties of the Indians, having their women and children with them and murdered many. Among these were, unfortunately, the family of Logan, a chief celebrated in peace and in war, and long distinguished as a friend of the whites."

This is certainly a *mitigation* of the charge against Capt. Cresap, but it leaves altogether indefinite the fact as to whether Greathouse and Cresap conjointly directed these parties, or which of the two murdered Logan's relatives. It relieves Cresap, however, altogether from the charge of murdering the Logan family *in canoes,* on the Kanawha, a fact which seems to have been current at Williamsburgh, Va., when the Abbe Robin was there and received the speech of *Lonan* from the "Williamsburgh professor.

It will be well for the reader to compare the speeches line by line as given by Mr. Jefferson and by the Abbe. The resemblances and the variances cannot fail to attract his critical notice.

This copy, if we admit the date to be the 11th November, 1774, as we have stated it to have been most probably, *is the eldest member of this family of speeches* I have been able to discover in tracing their pedigree. No *manuscript* copy of the time has, to my knowledge, ever been found.

III.

My friend Mr. Thomas H. Ellis, of Richmond, Virginia, sent me the following authentic copy of the message of Logan, extracted from the *Virginia Gazette*, No. 1226.

"WILLIAMSBURGH, *February* 4, 1775.

"The following is *said to be* a message from Captain Logan (an Indian warrior) to Gov. Dunmore, after the battle in which Col. Charles Lewis was slain, delivered at the treaty:

"I appeal to any white man to say that he ever entered Logan's cabin but I gave him meat; that he ever came naked but I clothed him. In the course of the last war Logan remained in his cabin an advocate for peace. I had such an affection for the white people that I was pointed at by the rest of my nation. I should have ever lived with them, had it not been for Colonel *Cressop*, [1] who *last year*, cut off in cold blood, all the relations of Logan, not sparing women and children. There runs not a drop of my blood in the veins of any human creature. This called upon me for revenge; I have sought it, I have killed many, and fully glutted my revenge. I am glad that there is a prospect of peace on account of my nation; but I beg you will not entertain a thought that any thing I have said proceeds from fear! Logan disdains the thought! He will not turn on his heel to save his life! Who is there to mourn for Logan? ..... No one."

IV.

From the IVth series of *American Archives*, vol. I, p. 1020, I extract the following:

"*New York*, February 16, 1775. Extract of a letter from Virginia: 'I make no doubt but the following specimen of *Indian* Eloquence and mistaken valour will please you; but must make allowance for the unskillfulness of the interpreter: [2]

"*The speech of* LOGAN — *a* SHAWANESE *Chief* — to Lord Dunmore:

"I appeal to any white man to say if ever he entered Logan's cabin hungry *and* I gave him not meat, if ever he came *cold or* naked and I *gave him not clothing? During the course of the last long and bloody war* Logan remained in his *tent* an advocate for peace; nay, such was my love for the whites, *that those of my own country pointed at me as they passed by, and said,* 'Logan is the friend of white men!' I had even thought to live with you, *but for the injuries of one man*. Colonel Cresap, *the last spring*, in *cool* blood *and unprovoked* cut off all the relations of Logan not even sparing my women and children. There runs not a drop of my blood in the veins of any human creature. This called *on* me for revenge. I have sought it — I have killed many — I have fully glutted my *vengeance. For my country I rejoice at the beams of peace ; but do not harbor the thought that mine is the joy of fear. Logan never felt fear.* He will not turn on his heel to save his life. Who is there to mourn for Logan? *Not* one."

---

1 He is here, in this message delivered in *October,* 1774, called *Colonel* Cressop, both title and name being inaccurately given. In the note left by Logan in the house in Virginia whose inhabitants he had murdered, dated 12th *July,* 1744, he styles him *Captain Cresap.* Thus he evidently knew his *proper* title *anterior* to the message in October, in which he miscalls him. That the title, if introduced at all, was assigned by Logan is unquestionable, for Gibson says Bo in his preceding testimony.

2 The Honorable William C. Rives, of Virginia, after receiving a copy of the first edition of my narrative, mentioned the following fact to me in a letter dated Castle Hill. 26th Sept. 1857:

* * * The copy " of the Logan speechj" published in the New York paper, which you have quoted from the 4th series of the *American Archives,* was sent by Mr. Madison to his friend William Bradford, of Philadelphia (afterwards attorney general of the United States), in a letter bearing date 20th January, 1775. This is proved by the extract given there of the letter from Virginia, which corresponds exactly with the language of Mr. Madison's letter of the above date, *now among his papers in my possession.* Mr. Madison in communicating the speech to his friend Bradford, says he had " *never seen it in print:* and yon will observe that his letter is dated two weeks before the publication in the *Williamsburgh Gazette.*

The variance of these two copies is not a little singular; the one published on the 4th Feb., 1775, at Williamsburgh, Va., and the other only fourteen days after, in New York, on the 16th of the same month in the same year.

The Virginia announcement states it to be only a *"message"* which was *"said to have been"* sent by *Captain* Logan (who was known to be a Mingo), to Lord Dunmore. The New York copy, during the transit from Virginia, is magnified into a Speech, and dignifies the orator as a "Shawanese Chief." Nor has the language of the document deteriorated by travel. The Indian abruptness and directness have been softened, and the reader will particularly note the variances which I have endeavored to point out by causing the chief passages to be printed in italics.

The next member of this eloquent lineage blooms in mature perfection, in the pages of Mr. Jefferson's *Notes on Virginia;* and, with its translation into French, in the year 1788, I shall close my analysis of the genealogy.

Mr. Jefferson says in his IVth *Appendix:* "the speech itself" was so fine a morsel of eloquence that it became the theme of every conversation, in Williamsburgh particularly, and generally indeed, where-so-ever any of the officers resided or resorted. I learned it in Williamsburgh; I believe at Lord Dunmore's, and I And in *my pocket book* of that year (1774), an entry of the narrative as taken from *the mouth of some person, whose name, however, is not noted nor recollected, precisely in the words stated in the Motes on Virginia:*

V.

"I appeal to any white man to say if ever he entered Logan's cabin hungry, and he gave him not meat ; if ever he came cold and naked, and he clothed him not. During the course of the last long and bloody war, Logan remained idle in his cabin, an advocate for peace. Such was my love for the whites that my countrymen pointed as they passed, and said : 'Logan is the friend of white men.' I had even thought to have lived with you, but for the injuries of one man. Colonel Cresap, 1 the last spring, in cold blood, and unprovoked, murdered all the relations of Logan, not sparing even my women and children. There runs not a drop of my blood in the veins of any living creature. This called on me for revenge. I have sought it : I have killed many : I have fully glutted my vengeance. For my country, I rejoice at the beams of peace ; but do not harbor a thought that mine is the joy of fear. Logan never felt fear. He will not turn on his heel to save his life. Who is there to mourn for Logan ? Not one." 2

VI.

"Y-a-t'il un homme blanc qui puisse dire qu'il soit jamais entré ayant faim dans la cabane de Logan, et a qui *Logan* n'ait pas donné à manger, et que *Logan* n'ait pas revêtu ! Durant le cours de la dernière longue et sanglante guerre, Logan est resté oisif dans sa cabane, exhortant *sans cesse ses compatriotes à la paix.* Telle étoit son amitié pour les blancs, que *ses frères*, le montrant au doigt en passant, disoient : ' Logan est l'ami des blancs.' *Il* vouloit même aller vivre *au milieu* de vous, avant qu'un homme le Colonel Cresap, au printems dernier, de sang froid et sans provocation, eût assassiné tous les parens de Logan, sans épargner même *les* femmes et *les* enfens. Ill ne coule plus maintenant *aucune* goutte de mon sang dans aucune créature vivante. J'ai voulu me venger ; J'ai combattu : j'ai tué beaucoup *de blancs.* J'ai assouvi ma vengeance. Je me réjouis pour mon pays *des approches* de la paix ; mais gardez vous de penser jamais que cette joie soit celle de la crainte. Logan n'a jamais connu la crainte : *Il ne tournera jamais ses pieds* pour sauver sa vie. Qui reste-t'il *maintenant* pour pleurer Logan ? Personne."

The slight variations in the translation are noted by italics.

Cresap was only a *captain;* but the translated Robin edition makes the felon a *major,* while Mr. Jefferson's elevates him into a *colonel,* though Logan had called him simply *captain* in his bloody *missive of 21st July,* 1774.

It will be observed with pleasure by those persons who are interested in the honor of Captain Michael Cresap's name, that the speech, as given in the "VIIth volume of our great national historian, Mr. Bancroft, published since the issue of the first edition of this narrative, does not charge Cresap with the Yellow Creek massacre, but omits his name entirely.

APPENDIX No. 3

The Speech and the Death of Tah-gah-jute or Logan

While the preceding pages have been passing through the press I had the honor to receive from Mr. Lyman C. Draper, the distinguished and indefatigable secretary of the "Wisconsin Historical Society, the following letters concerning the speech and death of Tah-gah-jute or Logan. The letters he quotes from his MS. collections are so interesting that I think historical students will be glad to receive and preserve them; and I have, therefore, added them at the end of this volume as illustrative of the story. I must record my great indebtedness to Mr. Lyman C. Draper for the communication of numerous facts and authorities, while I was occupied in the composition of this essay in 1851, and lately, also, while preparing the present edition. No student of American border life, in early days, has accumulated so large, various, and valuable a stock of original MSS. and printed authorities on the subject, as this kind and enlightened scholar. No one opens his treasures with more generosity to his friends and co-laborers. I may be permitted, also, to express the hope — in which, I am sure American historians will cordially unite — that Mr. Draper will soon commence the publication of that series of Pioneer Histories and Biographies, upon which, it is known, he has been employed for so many years.

Logan's Death.
"Pleasant Branch, Dane Co., Wis.,
May 20th, 1867.

"My Dear Colonel Mayer:

"I was yesterday looking over and assorting some of my old manuscripts, preparatory to a pasting process for binding, and I came across a notice of the last days of Logan that I had entirely forgotten, and thinking you might possibly still be able to use it, if you should desire to do so, I will copy and send it.

"In August, 1781, Maj. Charles Cracraft, of Washington Co., Pa., and twelve men, descending the Ohio, as a part of Gen. G. R. Clark's intended expedition against Detroit, were intercepted near the mouth of the Great Miami, by a large body of Indians, and made prisoners. Maj. Cracraft's son, Wm, Cracraft, has furnished me his recollections of his father's relation of his captivity and events connected therewith, and among them the following about Logan, which he communicated to me under date October 1st, 1853, by which you will perceive I did not possess it when you prepared and published your original work on Logan and Cresap in 1851. I will give it in the plain narrative communicated to me, and if you have occasion to use it you must put in shape: —

"'I think in my last letter to you mention was made of an acquaintance had by my father, at the time of his captivity with Alexander Macomb, a resident near Detroit, and father of the late Gen. Alex. Macomb, of the U. S. Army' [where (Mr. Cracraft mentions elsewhere), his father was ever kindly treated, and furnished with reading matter, to while away the tedium of his captivity, having given his parole not to run away, nor pass more than three miles beyond the limits of Detroit.] At that time, a certain William McMillen, who had been taken prisoner by the celebrated Indian chief and warrior, Logan, was in the employ of Mr. Macomb, working on his farm, and there my father became acquainted with McMillen, and learned from him much of Logan's life and history. It appears that Logan and McMillen had hunted together before the war; and McMillen was made prisoner by Logan and his party near Clover Lick, on the Greenbrier fork of the Great Kanawha River, Virginia, and taken to Detroit and retained there, and with the privilege of personal freedom by remaining in or near the post of Detroit. It appears that McMillen was a favorite of Logan, for the latter called often to see him, when returning to Detroit with scalps and prisoners.

"' I will give you as near as possible the relation given by my father as to Logan's death. Many years before my father's decease, I had read Jefferson's account of Logan with much interest, which accounts for my recollection of the narrative given me by my father. And now to the narrative:

"' It appears that Logan in one of his trips to Detroit, and I might say his last one, with scalps and prisoners, after having made disposition of them according to the then British regulations, got into an Indian drunken frolic and became so troublesome that Captain Bawbee, the commissary of the Indian department, kicked him out of the store-house. Logan took it in high dudgeon, and the next day he went to Mr.

Macomb's residence to hunt up William McMillen; and, after meeting him and passing the usual salutations, Logan said: 'Bill, I want to have a talk with you, and wish you to meet me at the Spring Wells, below Detroit,' signifying the time by pointing to where the sun would be in the horizon. McMillen acceded to his request and at the appointed time met Logan at the Spring Wells.

"Logan commenced by giving an account of the abuse he had received from the British at the hands of Bawbee. 'Bill,' said he, addressing McMillen, ' Why, Bawbee kicked me out of his house, and called me a dog! Bill, I won't fight for the British anymore; they have treated me very bad. Now, Bill, take this tomahawk, and tell how many prisoners, and how many scalps, I have taken from the Big Knives [the Virginians] for the British.' Logan had made a notch-record on one side of his hatchet handle for each prisoner taken, and on the other side for each scalp. McMillen said he counted them, and they exceeded seventy. 'Now, Bill,' continued Logan, 'I would go back to the Big Knives, if I thought they would not kill me, and would kill and take as many of the British as I have done of the Big Knives; but I dare not go. Bill, I can kill as many bucks as any Indian on the Scioto River; I will go home, and hunt deer, raccoon and beaver.' And, from the narration, it seems that Logan soon left Detroit for his home on the heads of the Scioto; and meeting some of his nation, on his journey homeward, who had some rum, he became "boosy" again, and then pursued his way to his camp; and in passing the Indian wigwam of the squaw whom he claimed for his cousin, he asked her for something to eat. She said they had nothing. Logan called her a liar, and took his wiping-stick or ramrod and gave her a severe whipping, calling her a lazy bitch, then mounted his horse and made off. The husband of the squaw coming home, and finding his wife still crying, and learning the cause of her trouble, and the course that Logan had gone, and knowing that he would have to make a circuitous route to avoid a swamp, took a nearer way, and got ahead of Logan, and lay in ambush until he came near, and then shot. At the crack of the rifle, Logan sprang from his horse, with his gun in one hand, while with the other he struck himself on the breast, at the same time advancing a few steps towards the place where the concealed Indian lay, exclaiming, 'I am a man!' and lie fell to the ground to rise no more. Thus ended the life of Logan, the once mighty Mingo chief and warrior whose name and acts had carried dismay and terror to the frontier settlers.

"So much for the Cracraft narrative... I see no reason to doubt its correctness, for I should think its details quite as reliable as any of the accounts we have of Logan's death, and much more circumstantial. Cracraft, the elder, was a major at the time of his captivity, and was a man of intelligence and observation, and is entirely worthy of credit. His son is equally worthy.

Logan's Speech

"Since I am on the Logan subject, I may as well give you copies of two statements I have with reference to the delivery of Logan's speech to John Gibson. The first is from the late chief justice, John B. Gibson, of Pennsylvania, a nephew of Col. John Gibson, and communicated to me by Judge Gibson in the form of a copy of a letter he had previously sent to the late E. D. Ingraham of Philadelphia:

"' Philadelphia, *21st Nov.,* 1846.

"*Dear Sir:* The facts you request are briefly these. The last time I saw General John Gibson, he related to me the circumstances of Logan's speech exactly as I had heard them from him before. He died a few months afterwards with his faculties unimpaired. The facts are, in substance, these: At the outbreak of what is *unjustly called Cresap's war —for Colonel Cresap had nothing to do with the murder of Logan's family, which provoked it —* Mr. Gibson, who had many years before been a prisoner for a long time among the Indians, attended Lord Dunmore in his expedition against the Indian towns, and speaking the Delaware tongue vernacularly, was sent into the principal one [village], with a flag, and an offer of peace. Midway he found Logan standing with folded arms, at the side of the path where it crossed a small stream, who to the salutation, 'How do you do, my friend, Log.? I am glad to see you,' sullenly replied, 'I suppose you are,' and turned away. On meeting the chiefs in council, Mr. Gibson was sorry to see that Logan was not among them; but while he was opening the terms of his mission, he felt himself plucked by the cape of his capote, and, turning, saw Logan at his back, with his face convulsed with passion, and beckoning to follow him. Logan rapidly led the way to a coppice outside the town, and, pointing to a log for a seat, burst into a torrent of tears. When he had regained the power of utterance, he pronounced the speech that has been the subject of so much discussion; with a view to remove from Lord

Dunmore's mind any doubt he might entertain as to the sincerity of the peace in consequence of Logan's refusal to take part in the treaty. At his return to camp, Mr. Gibson made an accurate translation of it, which, as it was much admired, was probably preserved by Lord Dunmore among the archives of the government. After the lapse of almost half a century, General Gibson would not assert that the speech published by Mr. Jefferson was a literal copy of his translation; but he was sure it contained the substance of it.

"'Here it is proper to remark, that he was as competent as Mr. Jefferson, or anyone else, to give it the simple dress in which it appears. But whoever was entitled to the merit of it, General Gibson said that it was a poor picture of the original, uttered, as it was, in accents dictated by an abiding sense of his wrongs, and in tones expressive of the hopeless desolation of his heart. It was its last passionate throb. The man was done with impulses, even of revenge. He sunk into apathy from intemperance, and in the course of a year was murdered in a drunken fray. It is some thirty years since I have seen the statement published by Mr. Jefferson, and know not how far it agrees with these particulars. They have ceased to be matters of interest; but they are probably the last that will be heard of poor Logan.

Very truly, dear sir,

Your obedient servant,

John Bannister Gibson.

'Edward D. Ingraham.'

"On receipt of the preceding I wrote to Judge Gibson, reminding him that Dunmore in 1774, had invaded the Shawnee country, and that it was evidently a Shawnee or Mingo town, not a Delaware one as he intimated, to which John Gibson had been sent, and he replied as follows :

"'Carlisle, *24th February*, 1848.

"*Dear Sir:* I have not the least objection to the corrections you propose. I know from particular circumstances, however, that General Gibson not only spoke the Delaware language, but that he used it in conversing with Logan. I was told many years ago by a person who was present at the trial of the distinguished Captain Samuel Brady, for killing Indians under belief that hostilities had commenced, that while General Gibson was interpreting the questions put to the Indian witnesses and their answers, one of them, then blind from age, asked the name of the Delaware chief who was then speaking. I was told also by General Gibson himself, that when he met with Logan on his way to the Shawanese town, he accosted him in his own language and, that to his surprise, Logan who spoke English very imperfectly and seldom when he could help it, replied to him in English. An impression received by me from the late missionary Mr. Heckewelder, is, that the Delaware language was the parent from which sprung the Mingo, Shawanese, and other tongues as dialects of it. I think it certain that the languages of these tribes are essentially the same. Logan, who adopted the name of one of the proprietary servants who was the father of the late Doctor Logan, of Germantown, was the son of Shikellemus, a Mingo chief, and the fast friend of the Penns, lived at an early day on an island in the Susquehanna at the mouth of the Juniata, where I saw the ruins of his cabin when I was a boy.

"'I was told by the late Judge Brown, now dead some thirty years, that Logan had frightened the settlement from its propriety by threatening to take the scalp of a man who owed him a few shillings but repudiated the debt. To prevent mischief, Judge Brown, who was then a justice of the peace, proposed to collect it for him; but Logan thought that if it was to be done by the arm of flesh, he was himself as competent to the task as anyone else. He, however, consented; and to his amazement, the money was recovered. He could not conceive how the power of the king could work such wonders at the distance of three thousand miles. He could no more comprehend the nature of delegated power than he could have comprehended the nature of the magnetic telegraph. He was, in truth, a mere savage, and his uncultivated eloquence, like poetry, only the concentrated language of feeling. I am ignorant of the date of his emigration to the banks of the Ohio.

"'Very truly, your obedient servant,
"'John B. Gibson.

"'Lyman C. Draper, Esq.'

"' Alleghany, *March 8th,* 1848.

"'J.W. Biddle, Esq.,

"'Dear *Sir:* I have put oft from day to day answering the enquiries of Mr. Draper in reference to Gen. Gibson's narrative of the circumstances under which the speech of Logan was delivered. In this case, it has been 'put off to a more convenient season,' as the daughter of Gen. Gibson is now on a visit at my house, and on comparing her remembrance with my own of the detail of that event, as given by her father, they correspond exactly.

" 'I shall, therefore, briefly state, that some thirty years since, on a visit to Braddock's Field, the residence of George Wallace, Esq., son-in-law of Gen. Gibson, where the latter made his home, Logan's speech became very naturally the subject of conversation as it was of deep interest. The general stated that at the delivery of the speeches of the whites at the council, Logan rose Up from the place where he had been sitting, and approaching Gibson, gave him a tug at his hunting shirt, and with an Indian's brevity said to him, 'Gibson, come;' in the act of moving off, another Indian begged him not to go, intimating that Logan might do him mischief. This, however, though delaying him for several steps behind Logan, did not deter him from following; and in this way they proceeded without Logan once ever looking round, for something like a mile, when they reached a thick copse of hazel bushes, into which Logan penetrated and Gibson after him, until they reached an old log, on which he beckoned the general to sit down.

"'At this time the general observed that Logan's agitation, with an evident effort to conceal it, was intense, and, in a moment, he burst into a flood of tears. He then soon resumed his composure, and proceeded to deliver the celebrated speech which has been the subject of so much remark and interest everywhere. The speech was delivered in his native tongue, for the general was familiar with the language, and an Indian never makes a speech in any other. And the general would no doubt have stated such an unusual fact, if it had been otherwise.

"'I knew Gen. Gibson from my earliest childhood; he was one of the most artless and unsophisticated men in the world, and the last man on earth that would make a false statement in narrating events. He was a pretty good English scholar, with a remarkable memory, yet without any fancy or imagination, though watchful and observant of all around him.

"'If you think this relation of sufficient interest, you can communicate it to Mr. Draper, and should be happy that I could be of any service in the matter.

"'I have written this in haste, and you must transcribe it so that it can be read.

"'*W.* Robinson, Jr.'

"The preceding, you will see, was addressed to the late Jas. W. Biddle, of Pittsburg, for me. I have copied rapidly so as to be in time for our mail. I feel sure you have now all I possess about Logan. I only wish it may be in time to be of service to you.

"Truly yours,

"Lyman C. Draper."

To Colonel Brantz Mayer, Baltimore."

INDEX

Clark, George Rogers, on the Ohio, with settlers, spring of 1774, 45; enrolls his band of men for protection, party fired on, 46; his letter concerning the Cresap and Logan controversy, addressed to Dr. S. Brown for Mr. Jefferson, and to correct Jefferson, 69.

Committee of Safety of Maryland arrest Connolly, 41; appoints Cresap captain, 61; its original papers in archives of Maryland Historical Society, 43, *note.*

Connolly, Dr. John, at Pittsburgh, 40; his arrest and examination at Fredericktown, Maryland, 41; his project to raise the Indians, 43, *note;* under Dunmore at Pittsburgh, 47, his message to G. R. Clark's party, 47.

Conoys, their hunting ground assigned 26.

Cornstalk, Indian chief, 118; treaty of, 81.

Cracrafts, account of Logan's death, appendix No. 3, 95, *et seg.*

Craddock, Rev. Mr., his school in Baltimore County, Maryland, 24; Cresap educated there, 24.

Craig, Neville B., concerning Logan's speech, 84.

Crawford, Valentine, Washington's land agent in the west, 1774, 44; letter to Washington, fixes date of Yellow Creek massacre, 49, *note.*

Cresap, Capt. Michael, date of birth, 24; taught at Rev. Mr. Craddock's school, Baltimore County, 24; runs away from school, whipped and sent back, 24; marries Miss Whitehead, and settled by his father as a trader, 24; unlucky, 24; fight with London agent in Fredericktown, 25; commences settling lands on the Ohio, 25; "Cresap's war," 36; on the Ohio in the spring of 1774,25; sent for by G. R. Clark's party, 45; counsels not to attack Logan's camp, 45; draws off his men, 46; Logan's letter to Cresap left at Roberts's after the murder, tied to a war club, 55; Cresap goes to Maryland, stopped at Catfish's camp (Washington, Pennsylvania), by a letter from Connolly, 56; Cresap commissioned by Lord Dunmore as captain in militia, Hampshire County, Virginia, 10 June, 1774, 56; Cresap returns to Maryland in autumn of 1774; in 1775 again went west and became sick, 60; returns towards Maryland, and is met by notification of appointment in the Rifle Corps, 61; Cresap's Rifle Company described in letter from Philadelphia, August 1775, 62; the skill of his men as marksmen; their hardihood, 62, 63; Cresap at Boston, joins American army 1775, 63; becomes ill, endeavors to reach home, dies in New York aged thirty-three, 63; buried in Trinity church-yard, N. Y., 1775, account of his funeral, 64, *note ;* his grave and grave-stone discovered by B. Mayer, in 1860, 64, *note;* facsimile of grave-stone and inscription, 68

Cresap, Col. Thomas, father of Michael,17.

Dah-gan-on-do, or Captain Decker, his narrative of Logan's death as lie received it from Tod-kah-dohs, 66.

Development, the progress of, the Discoverer, the Conqueror, Pioneer, Hunter, Farmer, Merchant, 12.

De Yong, the tailor, Logan's adventure with him, 31.

Doddridge, Rev. Dr., 16.

Draper, Lyman C, records Michael Myers's narrative, 50, *note;* his eminence as a historical student and scholar, 95.

Dunlop, James, letter to B. Mayer, concerning Logan's speech, 86.

Dunmore's, Lord, 39

Du Quesne, Fort, or Fort Pitt, or Pittsburgh, 14.

Dutch family, massacred on the Kanawha, 1773, 39.

Ellis, allowed to pass by the Indians because he was a Pennsylvanian, 38.

Emigration, tendencies of, 10.

Evans, Lewis, the geographer, travels with Bartram and Kalm, 1743, 28, *note.*

Fort Pitt, or Pittsburgh, 14.

French forts, 21.

1780,66; a marauder with Capt. Bird, 66 ; Logan's speech, different versions of, see appendix No. 2,88; evidence pro and con the speech, 81; Abbe Robin's copy of speech, 88: Barton's Medical and Physical Journal, 89, *note;* analysis of the speech, 90, etc.; version of Virginia Gazette, 91; Mr. Madison's copy, 92; Jefferson's copy, 94; a French copy, 94; Logan's death, various accounts of, 66, *note;* Vigne's Ohio Historical Collection, etc., account of his death, by Major Cracraft, appendix No. 3, 95; Logan disgraced by Bawbee, the Indian commissary, at Detroit, determines to fight no longer for the British, 96; had taken seventy scalps for the British in 1781, 97; whips his squaw cousin, and is slain by her husband, 97.

Logan, Dr. James, secretary of Pennsylvania, died 1751, 29.

Loudon's Indian Wars, 17.

Mack, brother, 26; his nephew at Shamokin, 1747, 27.

McClay, 29.

McClure, Rev. Mr., meets Logan near Fort Pitt, 33.

McComb, Alexander (Gen. McComb's father), at Detroit, 96.

McCurtin's Journal, notice of M. Cresap, 61, *note.*

McDonald, Major Angus, 56; march through the wilderness, 56: destroys Indian towns, 57.

McKee's account of Logan's speech, 88.

McMillen, William, Logan's prisoner at Detroit, 96.

McNitt, 29.

Map, by Col. T. Cresap, of the true fountains of the Potomac, in MS., in collection of Maryland Historical Society, 21

Map of Indian towns on Pickaway plains, 59, *note.*

Martin, a Virginian trader, and two companions, killed on the Hockhocking, 38.

Martin, Hon. Luther, attorney general of Maryland, distinguished federal politician, marries daughter of Capt. Michael Cresap, attacks Mr. Jefferson for his assault on his father-in-law's memory, 77.

Massachusetts laws as to bounties for Indians' scalps, 37; bounties paid for ten scalps, £1,000, 38; chaplains accompanied the attacking parties, 38.

Milestone, antique one, near Frostburg, Md., the inscriptions on its sides, 20, in *note*.

Milliken, Samuel, 29.

Mohicans, their hunting ground assigned, 26.

Monseys, their hunting ground assigned, 26.

Morrison, Major James, 76.

Myers, Michael, his narrative on the attack of Logan's camp, 107, 99, *et seq.*

Nanticokes, their hunting ground assigned 26.

Nemacolin, an Indian, and Col. Thomas Cresap, to mark the first road through the Alleghenies, 20.

New River, persons slain on, 37.

Norris, Mrs., her narrative, 32.

Ohio, the, the recognized boundary between the whites and Indians ninety years ago, 10.

Ohio Company, the, its grant from the king, 19.

Ohio Historical Collections, Howe's account of Logan's death, 67.

Sappington, John, his account of the Yellow Creek massacre, 51; he is the man who killed Logan's brother; McKee's certificate, 52, *note.*

Schmidt, Anthony, the blacksmith, sent from the Mission at Bethlehem to Shamokin, 27.

Settlements, the limits of the early, 13.

Seward, William H., Hon., secretary of state, verifies the letters of Brown and Clark, as to the Jefferson and Cresap controversy, as taken from the originals in the State Department, 77.

Shamokin, Indian village, site of, etc., 27, *el note;* modern Sunbury.

Shawanese, the, fail to comply with the treaty of 1764, 36; their name, 36, *note;* their murders and robberies, 38; their hunting ground assigned, 26.

Shikellamy, chief of a tribe at Shamokin, 26; alleged to be a Frenchman of Canada, 28, *note;* what he presided over, 27, *note;* notices of his sons and their deeds, 29, *note.*

Sinclair, Arthur, letter to Gov. Penn, 51.

Smith, Bevereux, to Dr. Smith, letter, 47, *note.*

Smith, James, 26, *note.*

Speech, Logan's, 59, characterized.

Spier's, 38; family murdered, 54, *note.*

Stag-dances and pioneer frolics at Red Stone Old Fort, 36.

Stone, William L., Life of Brant, 67.

Stroud, Adam, wife and seven children murdered, 38.

Stuart, Col., his narrative referred to, 57, *note.*

Susquehanna River valley, the, assigned as the hunting ground of the Shawanese, Conoys, Nanticokes, Monseys and Mohicans, 26.

Tah-gah-jute, or Short Dress, the Indian name of Logan; authority for, 29, *et note.*

Tod-kah-dohs, or the Searcher, his account of Logan's death, 66, *note.*

"Tomahawk improvement" — a mode of securing a title to land by girdling and marking trees, 34.

Tomlinson, Benjamin, account of Logan's speech, 84.

Tomlinson, Jacob, his account of the Yellow Creek massacre, 52, etc., *note.*

Treaty of Camp Charlotte, 57.

Vigne's account of Logan's death, 67.

Virginia's territorial claim, in 1774, 13.

Virginians butchered 38; twenty Virginians and the party robbed in 1771.

Virginia planters and Pennsylvania traders, animosities between, 40.

War of 1774, called Cresap's War and Dunmore's War, outbreak and causes of, 35, *note,* et seq., 22, *note;* summary of causes 23; campaigns and battles, 57, *note.*

Washington, George, land-holder on the Ohio, etc., 1774, 44, *note;* advertisement, 44.

Weiser, Conrad, 28; his opinion of Shikellamy, 29; he travels with John Bertram, Kalm and others, 1743, 30.

Wharton's Company waylaid and killed, 37.

Wheeler, Dr., 50, *note.*

Wheelock, Rev. Eleazer, memoirs of, 34, *note.*

Wood, Capt. James, interview with Logan, 1775, 64; journal of, 65.

Yellow Creek massacre, the, described, 54, et seq.

We hope you enjoyed this book. For more great stories from our past, please visit the Historical Collection at the web site.

Badgley Publishing Company

WWW.BadgleyPublishingCompany.com

www.ingramcontent.com/pod-product-compliance
Lightning Source LLC
Chambersburg PA
CBHW031518040426
42445CB00009B/292